God's Living Word

GOD'S LIVING WORD

by

ALEXANDER JONES, S.T.L., L.S.S.

DEUS BOOKS
PAULIST PRESS
(Paulist Fathers)
Glen Rock, New Jersey

24

Contents

Contents

Foreword

IN these days of biblical revival we must be sure that we are assisting not at an exhumation but at a true resurrection. For what will be the gain if we find the Word of God incorrupt as marble but without stir of breath or feature? Not that the cold business of critical analysis is to be despised: without it our understanding is arbitrary and we build on fantasy. But, grateful that these foundations have been truly laid in these last hundred years and more, our generation may begin where others have finished. It is the age of biblical theology. This is not to say 'systematic theology'; though we may synthesize for our own convenience, we find no such system in the Bible. The profound theology of St Paul himself is not an ordered treatise, it is a series of thrusts provoked by difficulties in his Churches or within himself. But what we lose in orderliness we gain in spontaneity and surprise. The Word is alive. Our problem is to tame it for observation without breaking its spirit. To do this, we must domesticate it, share our house with it, watch it discreetly as it grows; and sympathy must go with shrewdness. In plain words, our recovered interest in the Bible must be prudent, intelligent, devout. Prudent, to recognize and use the work already done; intelligent, to direct this work to the Scriptures' purpose which is to instruct and form the man of God; devout, to make sure we appreciate what we are handling—a sharp sword which is no less than the imperative Word of God.

Such sobering thoughts were in the author's mind when the Catholic Biblical Association of Australia invited him to conduct its first Biblical Congress in Sydney in the August of 1959. He went, though angels might have feared to tread. And for all his own shortcomings he had no moment of repentance: the warm heart of Catholic Australia saw to that. This book is in substance what he tried to say.

One must not weary the reader—if Forewords have readers—with a litany of thanksgiving. But certain kindnesses have no right of concealment. To His Eminence Cardinal Gilroy, first, I must say how grateful I am for the hospitality of his diocese and of his house. To Dr Harry Davis, that rare mixture of organizing ability and deep human kindness. To Fr Ian Sanders, bodyguard, and most ruthless chauffeur in Sydney. To Fathers Baker and Dalton, friends who seemed to me most typical of all the magnificent Australian priests it was my fortune to meet; to these and all the other members of the Biblical Association with its benign doyen, Monsignor William Leonard. To St Patrick's College, Manly, whose staff and students made a real home for me. To many other welcoming and welcome friends, and in particular to Mr and Mrs Pat Laming who made me one of their family. To those also in Melbourne, Perth, Brisbane, Newcastle who promoted series of lectures in their cities, and those who treated me so kindly. To all of these and to my patient audiences I beg to dedicate this book, asking God's blessing on the biblical movement in Australia's vigorous Church.

Mr Ronald Walls of Edinburgh most kindly undertook to reduce my chaotic papers to order. I thank him warmly for his help. The first chapter appeared in *The Bridge,* II, 1956, and is here reproduced by kind permission of Fr John Oesterreicher, its editor. One or two other chapters have appeared, whole or in part, in *Scripture,* and are here by permission of the editor, Fr Thomas Worden.

Alexander Jones,
Upholland.
January 26, 1961.

CHAPTER 1

The Word Is a Seed

OF even the richest languages it is true that for every million ideas there are only a thousand words. The colour range may serve as an example: no one will ever fit words to every shade of the spectrum— not a tongue is called for but a paint brush.

Now if this were the whole of it, we might well despair of expressing all but our most simple thoughts. But in truth there is no such thing as a pure note in the scale of human tongues; or, rather, each note summons its family of overtones, born to it in its years of history. The word the mother teaches her child was already venerable when she herself received it. It had grown old in the service of her ancestors; it had been sent on this errand and on that; at one time it had toiled in the cellars of literature, at another it had shone in its courts, adroitly adapting itself to all changes of fortune. After the experience of a hundred lifetimes this word, old but very vigorous, remained still itself but became so much more. And now it wears on its face the pain and the joy of its long story. We ourselves give it something, too; because having served with us it outlives us who seemed to be its masters. We pass. The word remains.

Now what if God should choose to take the word into his service? Supposing God were to use the tongue of man—what then? Plainly, no word will outlive him; nor did it exist before him. God foreknows the fortunes of his word. No part of its story (what we call past and present and future) is hidden from him. He sees it, therefore, with eternal eyes and knows it wholly—seed and flower and fruit. Should he send it to do his bidding, he already knows what will become of it. Man learns the varying power of the word only as generation succeeds generation; but God is aware of it from eternity. Or, if we may change the image yet again, the word that first appeared naked will reappear—since it is for man that God intends it —in the fashion of the generation to which it is revealed.

If, therefore, through the medium of written sentences God elects to reveal himself to man in one favoured millennium of history; and if—since God is a wise God—that revelation is tuned to the reception of its hearers; and if—because God is a God of truth—that revelation can never contradict itself as it increases in volume but must now cry aloud the self-same thing that once it whispered, then the thousand years of revelation is a period to be considered in its entirety, to be savoured only when it is complete. Then and then only can its first beginnings be seen as beginnings and the innate but latent power of the Word acknowledged. I do not know the acorn until I have seen the oak.

The Bible, then, is not a granite block of equal density throughout, immovable, undeveloping, dead. It is not like a coral reef growing in bulk through the years by the mere juxtaposition of homogeneous matter. It is the living word of the living God. It is a thing that grows from within, vitally. At no stage of its growth, therefore, can it be justly appreciated. We must wait until it has achieved full stature. After all, we can no more make an exploratory incision into living things without destroying the tissue than we can give ourselves time to admire the water's flow by freezing it. I say this with regard to the theme of the present essay but dare add, in passing, that it has wider application in a wider context. So much distortion of God's Word is born of the monstrous parentage we may call the static outlook. So often it is the Bible's misfortune to be taken for a series of adjacent oracles, each independent of the other and all independent of their setting, snatched out to vindicate the perpetuation of some passing stage of man's relation-

ship with God. There is no more fundamental error
in the whole range—and it is an alarmingly wide
range—of exegetical absurdities. In this way a man
could even justify the desert law of vendetta in our
modern cities, could build another Ark of the Com-
mandments according to the pattern shown to Moses
on the Mount, could make the thousandth year of
revelation look no different from the first.

For if the Word was not spoken idly to the fathers,
neither was it spoken only to the fathers. It was spoken also for our instruction 'upon whom the final age
of the world has come' (I Cor. 10:11). That the
Word still lived was the basic conviction of the
Church's earliest days. It has been very justly said,
indeed, that 'the application of prophecy was probably
the earliest form of Christian theological thought'.[1]
This theology, which precedes and underlies our New
Testament writings, is therefore a biblical theology in
the fullest sense of the phrase. The first duty of the
disciples was, no doubt, to inform the world of the
facts — of the suffering, death, and resurrection of
Jesus of Nazareth, 'a prophet mighty in work and
word' (Luke 24:19). But they had also to show their
Jewish brethren that this new Thing was no foundling
in Israel's cradle but the heir of all the prophets. To
the Gentile they had to show that the wisdom of Providence had not been silent before and had spoken freely
now. Old and New Testaments had to be brought together; the Word must be shown to be consistent with
itself—the Word at no time destroyed and now at
last fulfilled.

Whatever the New Testament writers meant by the
term 'fulfillment', they did not mean some mathemat-
ical equation of past promise and present performance. Far from it. For them the reality transcended

[1] C. H. Dodd, *History and the Gospel* (London: Nisbet, 1938),
p. 60. Dr. Dodd's statement is adequate as long as we remember
that the theological argument does not consist of an alignment
of texts selected from Old and New Tesaments. The argument
implicit in this present essay is of a very different kind.

the promise: Israel had expected a King; it had received a king of kings. With this in mind we may well hesitate before some popular forms of what is called 'the prophetic argument'—forms that would persuade us that the prophets wrote the gospel before the gospel. No, the vision of the prophets was obscure; they could hope only for a vague outline, peering out, as through a fog, to catch some sight of the period and pattern of messianic days.[2] This is why Christ could bless the eyes of his disciples, which looked upon the things 'many prophets and just men had longed to see' (Mt 13:16-17).

Even the formal assurance of prophecy, therefore, had its shortcomings. But we have more than this, much more. For it is the whole record of Israel's story that is God's word to man—an acted word, as truly conveying his meaning as does the visible universe. The pattern of this history not only recurs within itself but reappears in the fullness of time. And when it thus reappears it is not, as it were, larger; rather is it resumed on a higher plane, becoming more refined, assuming a spiritual nature.[3] It was thus that the Hebrew always looked upon his history. Unlike the Greek he never saw time as a series of wheels, each period powerless to grow beyond its own circumference, impotent to do aught but imitate its predecessor in rise, decline, return. For the Hebrew, as for the Christian, a driving Providence bears history along toward a goal. The movement is real and forward, not frustrated and cyclic.[4] Nevertheless, as we have

[2] Such is the clear impression left by St Peter when he speaks of the prophets' 'earnest inquiry and search' into the grace that was to come (1 Peter 1:10).

[3] One example is the 'March in the Desert' theme, taken up by the prophets and gathered into the New Testament. See J. Guillet, 'La Marche à travers le Désert', *'Recherches de Science Religieuse'* (1949), pp. 161-181; also Barnabas M. Ahern, C.P., 'The Exodus, Then and Now', *The Bridge*, I, pp. 53-74.

[4] C. N. Cochrane has reminded us again of St Augustine's repugnance for the theory of cycles, for history's moving like a wheel, which so utterly contradicts the Judaeo-Christian convic-

said, it is repetitive: the ascent goes on and the same obstacles recur to be conquered, though on a higher level. The summit is above the clouds.

About the Old Testament there hangs an air of something unfinished, and one feels that the Hebrew mind should be the first to sense it. In his heart's heart the Jew, son of patriarchs and prophets, cannot believe that God should halt where the Old Testament ends, and so he lives on deferred hope. Neither can the Christian believe it, but for him the New Testament provides insuperable climax. For the Christian the Old Testament and the New are movements of one great symphony, the one movement calling for the other. Without the New Testament the Old is a chain of melodies of great beauty — of melodious hints leaving us with a sense of loss, of lovely sounds cut off in their childhood. But without the Old Testament the New bursts upon the ear almost brutally, the ear being not yet attuned to the key or to the mode: the music is heard, but its great motifs are not fully recognized; its several parts are wondered at, but are not understood as the parts of one majestic whole. For the Christian the thin and separate melodies of the Old are in the New brought together, given richer tone, contrapuntally interwoven, discovered to have belonged all the time to one musical composition. And as foolish as it would be to deliver judgment on the sole witness of preparatory bars, so foolish does he hold it to pronounce upon either New Testament or Old without its fellow.

This sensation (for it is more than an impression) has a cause which is capable of literary proof. All the great themes of the Old Testament—and they are all 'words' of God: we might name at random the themes of the Presence, the Sacrifice, the Temple— work toward a sublime maturity they do not find ex-

tion that time and also space are not causes but opportunities, 'not gods but gifts'. See Cochrane, *Christianity and Classical Culture* (New York: Oxford Univ. Press, 1944), p. 484: *De Civ. Dei*, XII, 14-21 (P.L. 41: 360-372).

cept in the New.[5] Of such themes we shall examine one: the theme of the Word of God itself. It is the very term we apply to the Scriptures. If we pursue this theme to its end, it should be clear how, not in fantasy but quite exactly, we can say: 'The Bible is Christ'.

Scripture grows, ripens into Christ, is Christ, for the Word of God is a seed, This agricultural image is common to both the Testaments; though the actual phrase belongs only to the New, its spirit is that of both. What in one is life-giving water is the very germ of life in the other:

> As the rain and the snow come down from heaven,
> 　　and return no more thither,
> 　　but soak the earth and water it,
> 　　and make it to spring
> 　　and give seed to the sower and bread to the
> 　　　　eater:

> So shall my word be,
> 　　which shall go forth from my mouth:

> It shall not return to me void,
> 　　but it shall do whatsoever I please
> 　　and shall prosper in the things for which I sent it.
> 　　　　　　　　　　　　　　　　(Is 55:10-11)[6]

[5] See A. G. Hebert, *The Authority of the Old Testament* (London: Faber and Faber, 1947), p. 218; cf. pp. 199-238; H. H. Rowley, *The Re-Discovery of the Old Testament* (London: James Clarke, 1945), pp. 14-23, 202-215; and Albert Gelin, *The Key Concepts of the Old Testament* (New York: Sheed and Ward, 1955). A short essay on the Temple theme from this point of view may be found in A. Jones, *Unless Some Man Show Me* (New York: Sheed and Ward, 1951), pp. 136-145.

[6] In the Word of God infallibly executing his will, man is blessed. Hence Isaiah likens the Word to rain, so needed by the dry land, so obviously not under human control, so clearly a gift—a blessing, then, for field, beast and man. The thought of rain as a gift is stressed in the Jewish prayer book. In the

The sower went out to sow his seed. . . .
Now the parable is this:
The seed is the word of God.

(Luke 8:5, 11)

When we speak of the 'history of religion', what do
we mean? By 'religion' we mean the acknowledgment
of a relationship between the human and the Divine,
between the finite and the Infinite. Now, to establish
such a relationship, infinite power is necessary. But
have there not been many attempts by man to bridge
the infinite abyss between the finite and the Infinite?
Indeed, yet even these human gropings, the pagan
religions, would not have been possible had not the
infinite Hand moved first. Strictly speaking, then, the
history of religion is not so much, nor essentially, the
story of man's quest for God but of God's for man.

The story begins with man's creation—the making
of the bond between man and God. It proceeds with
man's growing recognition of this basic fact and of its
consequences for himself. Whence comes this recognition? From reason, we say. True, but not the
whole truth. It is reason indeed but reason working
on something intelligible. That intelligible thing is
man himself and the creation around him—contingent
things through which human reason attains to the
existence of the Necessary. In other words, by the
fact of creation God has *communicated* with man;

second of the Eighteen Benedictions, the devout Jew prays:
'Thou, O Lord, are mighty forever, thou revivest the dead, thou
art mighty to save.' From autumn to spring, from the day after
the feast of the Rejoicing of the Law till the eve of Passover, he
adds: 'Thou causest the wind to blow and the rain to fall.' See
The Authorized Daily Prayer Book, trans. and ed. J. H. Hertz
(New York: Bloch Publishing Co., 1952), p. 133. In connection
with this Benediction, the Talmud speaks of three keys that are
God's: the key of rain, the key of birth, and the key of the rising
of the dead—a beautiful thought even though the Talmud adds
that these keys are not entrusted to the hand of any messenger
(Ta'an. 2a; cf. *The Babylonian Talmud*, ed. I. Epstein, London:
Soncino, 1938, Ta'nith, p. 3).

creation is a Word of God to man—the first Word of
God to man.

The act of creation is therefore an act of speech,
of speech in a tongue understood by all who would
hear, a standing witness against all who would not:

> For from the greatness and the beauty of created
> things their original author, by analogy, is seen.
>   (Wisdom 13:5)

And again:

> The heavens declare the glory of God,
> and the firmament proclaims His handiwork.
> Day pours out the word to day,
> and night to night imparts knowledge.
>   (Ps 18:2-3)

The created universe, then, is a revelatory Word to
man; it is a thing that speaks to him, and in this the
two meanings of the Hebrew term *dabar* ('word' and
'thing') come together.

So much for man. But as it proceeds from God,
the Word not only speaks; it is also creative. When
God 'utters', an effect is necessarily produced. The
Greek *logos* and the Hebrew *dabar* may agree in their
dictionary meaning; in reality, since the two terms
are children of opposed mentalities, they are poles
apart.[7] For the Greek, the 'word', *logos,* is an instru-

---

[7] Thorleif Boman, in *Hebrew thought compared with Greek,*
(London, 1960) sums up this difference well. The noun *dabar*
comes from the verbs *dabar* and *dibber*, 'to speak'. But the root-
meaning is 'to thrust forward' and in consequence—picturing,
as it were, the act of speaking—'to let words follow one another'. Because of the basic meaning of the verb, *dabar* means
'deed' as well as 'word'. Eliezer's telling, for instance 'all he
had done' (Gen 24:66) is in Hebrew his telling all the 'deeds'
or 'words' he had done. But to say that the Hebrews made no
sharp distinction between word and deed is not to say that they
did not know words that promised much but were never acted
on. In such a case, the fault as they saw it was not that the
speaker brought forth only a word, and no deed. What he had
brought forth was an evil, empty, lying word, a word that lacked
the inner power and truth for realization. Never could a Hebrew

ment and expression of thought even if the thought remain unuttered. But when the Hebrew speaks of the 'word', *dabar,* he always thinks of something strangely operative; when he speaks of the Word of God, *debar Yahweh,* he is thinking of the expression of God's sovereign will and also of the vehicle of His irresistible power. This creative aspect of God's Word is never far from the Hebrew mind. Hence the book of Wisdom:

> God of my fathers, Lord of mercy
>   you have made all things by your word.
>   (Wisdom 9:1)

And the Psalmist:
> By the word of the Lord the heavens were made
>   by the breath of His mouth all their host.
>   (Ps 32:6)

These two facets of God's Word, the revelatory and the creative, will never be separated in Israel's literature—an ancient and momentous concept which the Christian revelation takes to itself, giving it climax and sublimity.

The act of creation, then is the first stage of God's

---

have burst out contemptuously, as Hamlet did: 'Words, words, words'. He could never, with Goethe's Faust, have called words *Schall und Rauch*; they were reality. To the Hebrew, then, the 'word-deed' is that which is highest and noblest in man. The Greek *logos,* on the other hand, derives from *legein,* 'to speak', the basic meaning of whose root, *leg,* is 'to collect', 'to order'. Hence, *legein* comes to have such diverse meanings as 'to count, to think, to say', *Logos,* having nothing to do with the function of speech, the dynamics of being-spoken, or the articulateness of speech, has to do with meaning, the ordered, rational content. And in this sense it represents to the Greek the highest human function. Compared, the two 'words' show what each people held most important in the life of the spirit: for the Hebrew it was the dynamic, lordly, majestic, powerfully creative; for the Greek it was the ordered, measured, carefully planned, and meaningful (pp. 52-54).

revelation to men, the initial epiphany of his 'Word'.
But it is only a beginning.

When God chose to shape a single people as the
organ of his message to the world, the Word became
more articulate. The voice of God sharpened, as it
were, into a series of specific commands addressed to
a nation: into the Sinaitic code which, in the most ancient legislative texts of the Bible is called 'the words'.
It is said, for instance, that the Lord would write upon
the Tables 'the words'; and again, that he wrote upon
them 'the words of the covenant, the ten words', *dibere
ha-berit 'aseret ha-debarim* (Ex 34:1, 28). The Word
written in the created heavens now comes to earth.
And though it commands, yet it is a kind, beneficent
word, for obedience removes all obstacles to the
Word's creative power, which will carry Israel to its
destiny. This is why Israel is bidden to follow the
voice of the angel of the Exodus—God's own mouth-
piece—if it would reach the Land. Israel's fortune
will always lie in following the Word, whatever form
it may assume.

The Word of the Law is more articulate than the
Word of creation; nevertheless it bears the same message of God's nature and demands. If the creative
Word already implied a divine law for man—a law
founded upon man's intrinsic dependence—it is no
less true that the legislative word is likewise creative.
It brings forth a light as real as, more real than, the
light that came when 'God said: "Let there be light,"
and there was light' (Gen 1:3). Hence the Law is a
light to the mind:

> A lamp to my feet is your word,
>   a light to my path.
>
> (Ps 118:105)

It does not surprise us, therefore, when the Psalmist
passes without apology from praise of the sun to praise
of the Law. Sun and Law are each a Word of God:

> He has pitched a tent there for the sun

which comes forth like the groom from his bridal
   chamber
and, like a giant, joyfully runs it course. . .
The law of the Lord is perfect,
   refreshing the soul . . .
   rejoicing the heart . . .
   enlightening the eye.

(Ps 18:5,6,8,9)

Here creation and legislation are side by side, products of the Word which is light to the outer and to the
inner eye. Again, the same Word that rules the universe rules God's people:

He sends His word and melts (the frozen waters);
   He lets His breezes blow and the waters run.
He has proclaimed His word to Jacob,
   His statutes and His ordinances to Israel.

(Ps 147:18-19)

But the Word is not exhausted in the ten words of
the Decalogue nor confined to the restrictive 'Thou
shalt not!' On the contrary. Long before the Exile,
'the Word' had come to stand for God's great favour
to His people—His self-manifestation by which each
might live. There is nothing cold, narrow, or legalistic about it; rather it is an abundant source of life:

It is something very near to you
   already in your mouths and in your hearts;
   you have only to carry it out. . . .
It means your very life.

(Deut 30:14; 32:47)

So much is the Word the life of the people that the
silence of Yahweh is, for the earliest of the prophets,
the most dreadful of all the punishments that could
befall it:

I will send forth a famine into the land:
   not a famine of bread,

nor a thirst of water,
but of hearing the word of the Lord.

(Am 8:11)

How could the absence of his Word not have been
the dread punishment it was, since Israel's God is the
'God who speaks'? And as sacred history goes on,
the Hebrew idea of the Word grows warmer and
richer so that one begins to wonder what divinely intended goal can satisfy this almost unconscious thrust.
Psalm 118, which has so often been most unjustly
taxed for 'its legalistic spirit', is in reality radiant with
love: it is perhaps *the* glorification of the Word in the
Old Testament, its highest praise. 'I hope in your
word' is its keynote. For 'your word, O Lord, en-
dures forever; it is firm as the heavens'—a phrase
that recalls Jesus' own: 'The heavens and the earth
pass; my word shall not pass.' And the Word which
is promise and precept is 'sweet to the palate; sweeter
than honey'. 'How deeply do I love your word!' is like
a refrain which, in many variations, runs through the
whole psalm.[8] It is important to note the entrance of
this element of affection, of profound love, because if
ever the Word is to be 'fulfilled', Israel will surely expect it to be supremely lovable.

As the 'Word', this medium of God's contact with
Israel, runs its course, it gradually becomes an object
of worshipful reverence—not indeed for its own sake
but because it is God's. The very fact that it has assumed two forms, creation and the Law, demonstrates
that it is independent of either and is free to assume
a third. Certainly we are far from Stoic philosophy,
in which the *logos* was no more than the inner pattern,
the intrinsic order and intelligibility, of the self-revealing cosmos. The Hebrew *debar Yahweh* is quite clear-

[8] Psalm 118: 74, 89, 103; and many other verses of the same
psalm. An excellent vindication of the truly devotional spirit of
Psalm 118 (in the Hebrew Psalm 119) will be found in A.
Rober, P.S.S., "Le Psaume CXIX et les Sapientiaux," *Revue
Biblique*, XLVIII (1939), pp. 5-20.

ly detached from any created thing; is it in any sense
whatever distinct from God? There is no doubt at all
that such an unexpected distinction confronts us in
the inspired poetic literature. And, in truth, this process of personification is far from alien to the concrete
mode of Hebrew thought. Though it does occur notably in the hellenistic period and reveals a certain
Greek influence, the process is authentically Hebrew,
for already in the Psalms the attributes of God are
poetically endowed with personality. God's attributes
of mercy and justice, of kindness and truth, are pic-
tured as two soldiers of the royal guard stiffly march-
ing:

Kindness and truth go before you.

(Ps 88:15)

Justice and peace are said to kiss, truth to spring out
of the earth, and justice to look down from heaven
(Ps 84:11-12). The Word is similarly endowed, and
since it can scarcely be described as an 'attribute', its
personification becomes all the more striking. Thus
it goes forth as a messenger, not an idle one, but one
that fulfils the errand that sped it on its way:

So shall my word be,
    which shall go forth from my mouth;
It shall not return to me void,
    but shall do whatsoever I please.

(Is 55:11)

Even more significantly, it reappears in the book of
Wisdom as a warrior of God destroying the firstborn
of the persecutor:

Your all-powerful word from heaven's royal throne
    bounded, a fierce warrior, into the doomed land,
    bearing the sharp sword of your inexorable de-
    cree.   (Wisdom 18:15-16)

The process goes on when Israel begins to identify

debar Yahweh, in which are all the treasures of wisdom, with the wisdom so eagerly sought in the Greek
world. Indeed, long before, in the book of Proverbs
(about the fifth century B.C.), Israel had identified
the Word—which is the Torah—with the Wisdom
the sage so perseveringly commends. In the much
later book of Wisdom (middle of the first century
B.C.) this identification is explicit:

> You . . . have made all things by your word
>   and in your wisdom have established man
>   to rule the creatures produced by you,
>   to govern the world in holiness and justice.
>   (Wisdom 9:1-2)

But it should be noticed that this Word-Wisdom of
the Hebrew is not, as it was for the Greek, the achievement of man but the gift of God. True Wisdom
dwells in heaven; if it is to come to earth God must
send it. What man has gone up to heaven to bring it
down from the clouds? asks Baruch (3:29).

Because of the identification of the Word with
Wisdom, the frequent personifications of Wisdom in
the books of the inspired scribes of Israel are perti-
nent here, for they are personification—however poetic—of the Word itself. This Wisdom-Word appears
in public like a prophet preaching in Jerusalem's
streets:

> On top of the heights along the road,
>   at the crossroads (Wisdom) takes her stand;
>   by the gates at the approaches of the city,
>   in the entryways she cries aloud.
>   (Prov. 8:2-3)

Wisdom claims eternal companionship with God before the world was, claims fellowship with Him in the
work of creation, claims to hold within itself the very
sources of life:

> From of old I was poured forth,
>   at the first, before the earth. . . .

When He made firm the skies above,
  when He fixed fast the foundation of the
    earth. . . .
then was I beside Him as His craftsman,
  and I was His delight day by day. . . .
He who finds me finds life.

(Prov 8:23,28,30,35)

This life it offers to men; the Wisdom-Word offers its
own self as the ever-sustaining food:

Come, eat of my food
  and drink of the wine I have mixed.

(Prov 9:5)

The fathers of Israel were ever being reminded that
'not by bread alone does man live, but by every word
that comes forth from the mouth of the Lord' (Deut
8:3). Their children too were ever being assured
that this Word would never cloy but would give increase of appetite:

He who eats of me will hunger still,
  he who drinks of me will thirst for more.

(Ecclus 24:20)

Are not these words somehow heard again on the lips
of him who sorrowed: 'You are not willing to come to
me that you may have life' (John 5:40); who stood
and cried out:

If anyone thirst,
  let him come to me and drink.

(John 7:37)

On his lips there is also the claim, couched in the very
terms of Ecclesiasticus and yet infinitely bolder:

He who comes to me
  shall not hunger,
and he who believes in me
  shall never thirst.

(John 6:35)

When a man comes who says: 'I am the bread of life'
(John 6:35), it is evident to the Hebrew mind what
he is claiming to be.

We have witnessed a tendency in Israel's sacred
literature to contemplate the Word of God as in a way
distinct from God; to consider it, with poetic—no,
more than poetic—imagination, as a person. The
post-biblical Jewish tradition went further still on the
way toward the personification of the Word. The
author of the book of Sirach had written that the Word
which came 'from the mouth of the Most High' was
created 'before all ages, in the beginning' (Ecclus
24:3, 9). He was speaking of the everlasting Wisdom. Rabbinical tradition took up the theme. The
Torah, it said, was made before the world was made,
the working tool of the Holy One for its creation:
God's perfect daughter, it was light, life, and truth.[9]

A no less honoured place was given to the Word
by the Targumim, the Aramaic renderings of the Old
Testament, whose oral tradition dates back to long
before Christ, though their final redaction was not
made till centuries after him. Now the Word is called
memra.[10] At first glance Memra would seem to be but
a respectful synonym for God. It is, as we shall see,
much more than this; yet it is indeed a literary device
to safeguard the divine transcendence, a 'buffer word',
as George Foot Moore has called it.[11] Thus it is no

[9] References in Gerhard Kittel, *Theologisches Wörterbuch
zum Neuen Testament* (Stuttgart: W. Kohlhammer, 1933), IV,
p. 139, lines 14-27.

[10] To be more specific, the Targumim use two terms for
'word': *pitgama* where the Hebrew Scriptures have *debar Yahweh*, 'the word of the Lord', be it revealing, prophesying, or com-
manding; and *memra*, which the Aramaic translators introduced
into the text to take the place of Yahweh, of God Himself. See
R. D. Middleton, 'Logos and Shekinah in the Fourth Gospel',
Jewish Quarterly Review, XXIX, 2 (Oct. 1938), pp. 107-108.

[11] George Foot Moore, *Judaism in the First Centuries of the
Christian Era* (Cambridge: Harvard University Press, 1944), I,
p. 419.

longer God who feels and tastes and handles, who is angered and takes offence; it is his Memra that does and suffers all these things. So the Targum to Gen 3:8 does not read: 'They heard the sound of the Lord God walking in the garden'; rather: 'They heard the sound of the Memra walking in the garden.' In the Targum to Deut 9:3, it is not the Lord God, it is his Memra, that is called 'a consuming fire'. Again, it is not Yahweh, the Lord God, it is his Memra, that regrets having created man, that smites all the first-born of Egypt, that is offended by Israel's grumblings in the desert.[12]

In these and other instances, Memra may well be a literary device to avoid speaking of God in too human terms. Yet there is a startling rabbinic insistence on the Memra's mediatorship between God and man. 'The Memra brings Israel near to God and sits on His throne receiving Israel's prayers', reads the Jerusalem Targum to Deut 4:7. Other targumic passages speak of the Memra as God's agent in the creating of the earth, in the administering of justice, in the ruling of man's destiny. Still others see the Memra as the shield of Noah and of Abraham, as the guardian of Jacob and of all the house of Jacob. Again, the Memra works the wonders of Egypt, goes before Israel in the desert, blesses the people and battles for it. It is called 'comforter' and 'witness' and 'like a father to Israel'. In the Memra 'redemption will be found'. 'My Memra', says the Lord God, 'shall be unto you like a good ploughman who takes off the yoke from the shoulder of the Oxen'.[13] These beautiful passages

[12] Targ. to Gen 6:6; Pseudo-Jon. to Ex 12:29; Targ. to Ex 16:8.

[13] The locations of the Memra passages are as follows: On creation, etc.—Targ. to Is 45:12; Targ. Jer. to Num 33:4; 27:16. On Noah's shield, etc.—Targ. Jer. to Gen 7:16; Targ. to Gen 15:1; 28:20-21; 35:3; Targ. Jer. to Ex 12:23, 29. On the wonders of Egypt, etc.—Targ. Jer. to Ex 13:8; 14:25; 20:1; Targ. Jer. to Num 23:8; Targ. to Jos 3:7; 10:14; 23:3. On the comforter, etc.—Targ. to Is 66:13; Targ. Jer. to Jer 29:23; 31:9. On redemption—Targ. to Zach 12:5. On the good ploughman—

leave no doubt that the targumic literature regarded the Word as a mediator between heaven and earth. Here, clearly, is an attempt to build a bridge between the finite and the Infinite, and we receive the impression that something new has been seen. Or better, the vision of God seems somehow fuller and richer; he is the God utterly transcendent and yet utterly immanent,[14] very far and very near. Moreover, the work of mediation between God and man is a divine work, given to the divine Word, the Memra, which issues forth from God.

Certainly the way is paved here for St John's presentation of Christ as the Word and for St Paul's presentation of him as the Wisdom of God (see I Cor. 1:24, 30; Col. 2:3). A Christian would suspect that here Jewish tradition was under pressure from revelation.[15] At the least the targumic use of Memra was a

Targ. to Os 11:4. For a fuller treatment see 'Memra', *Jewish Encyclopedia*, VIII, pp. 464-465.

[14] Well worth recording is J. Abelson's view that the chief reason behind the use of Memra is the desire to express God's immanence. 'The view commonly taken that the Memra is an expedient for avoiding the ascription of anthropomorphism to the Deity is only half the truth', he writes, for 'the Memra has a deep theological or mystical significance', entering 'into the relations between the human and the Divine, between God, man and the world, to an even greater extent than the *Shechinah*'. The Memra, Abelson states, 'is the expounding of the "Word" from the Jewish point of view. All things exist by virtue of the word (i.e. Memra) of God. It permeates everything, brings everything into the realm of being, conditions everything. It is the immanent manifestation of God in the world of matter and spirit. Divine wisdom, Divine power, Divine love, Divine justice, all these do not abide in the highest heavens, isolated, unapproachable, unknowable. They are embedded in the scheme of things we can see and feel and touch and know. They are a part of the constitution of man and the world. Man and the world are a fragment of them. The Memra comprises and expresses these teachings.' *The Immanence of God in Rabbinical Literature* (London: Macmillan, 1912), pp. 150-153.

[15] L. Bouyer rightly calls attention to the importance of this post-biblical tradition in *La Bible et l'Evangile* (Paris: Les Editions du Cerf. 1953), pp. 251-255. See also L. Hackspill, 'Etude

psychological preparation for the shock of Christ's newness; in this sense too Memra may be called a 'buffer', but a 'buffer idea' rather than a 'buffer word'. Quite evidently, and understandably, Jewish faith in the one living God—a faith so often imperilled by the polytheistic world around it and by the people's temptation to compromise with that world—would have been affronted by a brusque 'I am God' from Jesus' lips. But the Memra might well say: 'I and the Father are one' (John 10:30), or: 'Philip, he who sees me sees also the Father' (John 14:9).

Yet an anxiety to combine God's remoteness above the universe with his proximity to his people Israel does not account for all the uses of Memra. This anxiety may well have led to the adoption of the term but scarcely explains its subsequent expansion—I mean its use in cases where no anthropomorphism is to be feared. The Targum to Deut 33:7, for example, reads not: 'Hear, O God', but 'Hear, O Memra of God, the voice of Judah's prayer'. Or again, the Jerusalem Targum to Num 10:35-36 which had Moses plead: 'Arise, O Memra of the Lord . . . Return, O Memra of the Lord.' Memra, then, is more than a literary device, more than a 'buffer'.

To say, as Moore does, that Memra 'is purely a phenomenon of translation, not a figment of speculation',[16] is perhaps to offer too sharp an alternative—an alternative which takes little account of the psychology behind a growing tradition. It would surely be rash to contend that the rabbinic tradition was setting up, side by side with the one God, a distinct creative and law-giving Person, itself divine in nature, even though the Targum to Gen 28:20-21 had Jacob vow, on the morning following his vision at Bethel: 'If the Memra of the Lord be my help . . . the Memra of the Lord shall be my God.' On the other hand, the insistence and persistence and extension of

sur le milieu religieux et intellectuel contemporain du Nouveau Testament. 3. La Parole de Dieu'. *Revue Biblique*, XI (1902), pp. 58-66.

[16] Moore, *op. cit.*, I. p. 418.

the extraordinary use of Memra seem to betray a need in Israel's soul comparable to the yearning of the prophet that God would rend the heavens and come down (Is 64:1). Hence, for instance, the repeated angelic interventions in the Jewish apocalypses of the same period. After all, it was that epoch of Greek speculation which sought intermediaries between finite and Infinite; the Jewish mind must have felt the influence. Further, it seems highly probable that the loving use of Memra in the targumic literature was later thought to come too close to Christian teaching —this would explain its suppression by the rabbinic commentaries on Scripture, the Midrashim, which followed the Targumim.[17]   If this suggestion is valid, then the Memra must have stood on the threshold of personification. I do not contend that Jewish tradition really knew whither it was tending but rather that there may have been a half-conscious thrust toward an unseen goal.[18]

[17] Such is the view of Kaufmann Kohler, who ends his article on 'Memra' in the *Jewish Encyclopedia* by saying: 'Possibly on account of the Christian dogma, rabbinic theology, outside of the Targum literature, made little use of the term "Memra" ' (VIII, 465).

[18] This position is midway between the two extremes: Memra a mere synonym for God, a device of translation devoid of all theological content; or Memra a person intermediary between God and man. In support of 'mere synonym', see Moore, *op. cit.*, I, pp. 417-419; and 'Intermediaries in Jewish Theology', *Harvard Theological Review*, XV (1922), pp. 53-54; Strack-Billerbeck, *Kommentar zum Neuen Testament* (München: C. H. Beck, 1922), II, pp. 303-304; W. F. Albright, *From the Stone Age to Christianity* (Baltimore: John Hopkins, 1940), pp. 286 ff.; J. Bonsirven, S.J. *Le Judaïsme Palestinien* (Paris: Beauchesne, 1934), I, pp. 216-217; J. Lebreton, *History of the Dogma of the Trinity* (London: Burns Oates, 1939), I, pp. 121-123, 162-163; and V. Hamp, *Der Begriff 'Wort' in den aramäischen Bibelübersetzungen* (München: Filser-Verlag, 1938), a complete examination of the targumic literature dealing with this subject. Against this position, see Middleton, *loc. cit.*, pp. 107-113; Bouyer, *op. cit.*, pp. 35-37; W. J. Phythian-Adams, *The People and the Presence* (London: Oxford University Press, 1942), p. 177.

To sum up: The Word of God in biblical thought reveals. It reveals whether by creation or by more direct instruction, which breaks in upon man from without. For the Greek, the Word, *logos,* was the inner order and reason determining the self-revealing cosmos, whether a personal God was to be thought of or no. It was not so, it could not be so for the Israel of old with its deep sense of the otherness of God, a sense we Christians inherit. Pantheistic thinking was as alien to the ancient people of God as it is to us. The Word, we have seen, became more and more articulate: the voice of creation was reinforced by the voice of the Law, the voice of the Law by the tongues of the prophets and of the inspired scribes. Finally, the notion of the Word reached a stage beyond which it could not go unless in truth it appeared in person upon earth. At this stage Israel stops, the Church goes on.

In the first chapter of the fourth Gospel, the final step in the long march is taken: 'And the Word was made flesh.' The Word that had spoken to man from rock and river; the Word that had alighted on Sion and spoken to Israel through the Law; the Word that had been spoken by the lips of the prophets; the Word that Israel's scribes and rabbis had reverenced as its guide and protector; this same Word—said the Evangelist—had this time, this end of time, taken to itself a human body.[19]

In a certain sense this Word had taken to itself many human bodies when it spoke through the prophets,[20] but now by a unique, permanent, and

[19] I use 'human body' here in the same way as the Evangelist uses 'flesh', for the whole of human nature, soul and body, with the emphasis on what is its infinite distance and difference from God: its mortal frailty.

[20] In the books of the prophets we read: 'The word of the Lord came to Isaiah, saying . . .' (38:4), or 'to Ezekiel' (1:3), or 'to Hosea' (1:1). But nowhere in the New Testament do we read that 'the Word of the Lord came to Jesus, saying . . .,' because it is *in* Him.

personal union it had assumed a human nature as its
instrument, as the new vehicle of revelation, speaking
as neither creation, nor Law, nor prophet could ever
speak.

It is needless to say that we men are incapable of
understanding God's Word as it is in him. It must be
mediated through the words of a human intelligence.
Hence the humanity assumed by the *Dabar,* the *Logos,*
is a true human nature, not an appearance only, and
its intelligence functions in truly human fashion—
otherwise the Incarnation is not the link between God
and ourselves. Nevertheless 'the Word was God'
(John 1:1). The Word was no second God any more
than the 'Word' of Jewish tradition had been, but the
Godhead was now seen to bear within itself a mystery
of plurality in unity—plurality of relation, unity of
essence—or, in the formula of a Christian theology
no less tenacious of monotheism than the Jewish: one
in nature, more than one in person.[21]

It was, if I may call it so, the paroxysm, the climax
of divine effort that brought the Word in the flesh.
The creative Word in the cosmos had been ignored
by the Gentile, 'who from the good things seen', the
author of the book of Wisdom mourns, 'did not suc-
ceed in knowing him who is' (13:1). The revealing

[21] Without discussing here certain of his misinterpretations
of St John's Gospel, it is interesting to note that Abelson (*op.
cit.,* pp. 161-165) finds nothing in St John's theology to counter
ancient Jewish tradition. To the Evangelist, who, according to
Abelson, echoes 'the Jewish apocalyptic as well as the Palestinian
rabbinic teachings in the first century A.D.', the truth that God
is one, that there is no 'dualism of Deity', is an 'unassailable
stronghold'. In the passage, 'The Word was with God, and the
Word was God. He was in the beginning with God. All things
were made through Him, and without Him was made nothing
that has been made', Abelson sees but a firm insistence on the
divine unity. I fear, however, that he did not discern the full
meaning of his own words when he spoke so rightly of the unity
of God as 'unique', 'incomparable'. For the oneness of God is a
oneness which breaks open our everyday thoughts and terms, a
unity absolutely above any unity to be met in the world of finite
creatures; it is a unity on an infinite plane.

Word in the Law had so often gone unheeded; that
Israel had not heard had so often been the lament of
the prophets (Is 1:3; 30:12; Jer 6:10; Ez 3:7; Os
9:17; Soph 3:2). And so the Word that spoke through
the prophets speaks again, this time through the Son,
speaking truly with human lips but most poignantly
in deeds. Of old, God had repeatedly declared his
love for his people, repeatedly shown it in Israel's
history. Yet it was still possible for men to ask how
far that love could go—perhaps even to begin to wonder what 'love' meant at all in an infinite God. But
now, translated into the sacrificing life and sacrificial
death of the Son, God's Word is shown to be a message of love as man understands love. Translated
into the resurrection of that crucified flesh, it is shown
to be a Word of triumphant hope and the promise of
life. For it is the function of the Word-in-flesh to
bring life, to create.

This is why the opening phrase of John's Gospel is
a deliberate echo of the first word of the Bible: 'In the
beginning', *Bereshith,* which is the very title of Genesis
in the Hebrew canon. There 'In the beginning' introduces an account of the creation of the material universe, and St John invites us from the outset to identify the Word which is to take flesh with the creative
Word of Israel's tradition:

> In the beginning was the Word. . . .
> and without him was made nothing.
>
> (John 1:1, 3)

This strikes the Psalmist's note:

> By the word of the Lord the heavens were made;
> by the breath of His mouth all their host. . . .
> For he spoke, and (the earth) was made;
> He commanded, and it stood forth.
>
> Ps 32:6, 9.)

And indeed the whole pattern of John's prologue,
which begins in heaven where 'the Word was with

God', then comes to earth where 'the Word was made
flesh', where it does its work of grace and creates the
new sons of God, urgently recalls the Isaian description of the Word as the rain coming down from above
to water the earth that seeds may grow and men live
(55:10-11). Again, the Word's descent is modelled
on the Old Testament hymns to the Wisdom which is
the Word: Wisdom with God from the beginning.
Wisdom taking part in the world's making, Wisdom
coming to earth to bestow its riches upon those who
would receive them.[22] Similarly, according to John,
the Dabar is 'in the beginning with God'; by him all
things were made; once more 'he came unto his own',
to the chosen people on earth, and gave to 'those who
believe in his name' 'the power of becoming sons of
God'.[23]

But the prologue of John is more than a prologue;
it is in miniature his own Gospel, in which there recurs constantly the theme of the Dabar which creates.
We may not agree with those who, on the model of the
Genesis account of creation, would arrange the whole

[22] Read the hymns in praise of Wisdom in Wis 9:9-12; Prov
8:22-32; Ecclus 24:5-31. See also C. Spicq, 'La Siracide et la
structure littéraire du Prologue de Saint Jean', in *Mémorial
Lagrange* (Paris: Gabalda, 1940), pp. 183-195.

[23] It may be well to remember that John was nurtured not
only on the Hebrew Scriptures but on their Aramaic versions as
well. Hence the prologue of his Gospel, illumining the mystery
of Jesus, has a savour also of the Targumim. For instance, as
'all things were made through Him', so, according to the Targumim, the world was created, the earth shaped, and man made
in God's image, by the Memra of the Lord (Targ. to Deut 33:27:
Targ. Pseudo-Jon. to Is 45:12; Targ. Jer. to Gen 1:27). Again,
as the Word-made-flesh 'dwelt among us', so according to the
Targumim, the divine presence (*shekinah*, in Aramaic *shekinta*)
was to dwell in the tabernacles of Shem and in the midst of
the children of Israel. (Targ. to Gen 9:27; Targ. to Ex 29:45).
And as John saw 'the glory as of the Only-begotten of the Father',
so the Targum has Moses, Aaron, and the elders of the people
see the glory (*kabod*, in Aramaic *yekara*) of the God of Israel
(Targ. to Ex 24:10).

of John's Gospel in a seven-day framework [24] but at least it is evident that the motif of new creation underlies every chapter of it.[25] The giving of life preoccupies it: 'I came that they may have life', 'I am the resurrection and the life', 'Unless a man be born again . . .' (10:10; 11:25; 3:5). Forty times the noun 'life' occurs in John's Gospel, to Mark's four. For John, Christ's is a new world, a creation of higher order than this, an order in which even the material body is glorified. It is the 'regeneration' or 'second genesis', the *palingenesia,* of which Christ himself speaks (Mt 19:28), the 'new creation in Christ' of Paul (Gal 6:15), the 'new heavens and new earth' promised by Isaiah (65:17) and seen near by John (Apoc 21:1). The turning point of history is come: the Word of the Lord, the *debar Yahweh,* has resumed its creative activity on a higher plane. Its is a destiny worthy of the God from whom it came.

It is not that a stray sentence here or there in the prophets glows more brightly in the light of Christ, but that the total expectation of Israel, increasing in tempo, growing in volume, rising in pitch, could never be thwarted—because it was of God. If there is one datum that stands out in the preaching of the ancient prophets, it is that God would do greater things for His people than the great things already done. But since it is of God we speak, the word 'great' must not be thought of in terms of size and visibility. In such a context true crescendo is of quality. However invisible its effect, the Word of God that raises creature to supernature is more powerfully active than the same Word when it first constituted creation in its natural being. In this is the Word 'fulfilled', that it has established man in the noblest state he is capable of receiving. It has not disappointed Israel's highest hopes in the God whose spirit 'renews the face of the earth' (Ps. 103:30).

[24] M. E. Boismard, *Le Prologue de saint Jean* (Paris: Editions du Cerf, 1953), p. 136.

[25] C. H. Dodd, *The Interpretation of the Fourth Gospel* (Cambridge: Cambridge University Press, 1953), pp. 294-296.

This, then, is the course the Word of Yahweh runs: from creation to creation, from making to remaking, from the fashioning of the world to the renewal of man, and even of the world in Christ. While marvelling at this journey, I am reminded of an old Jewish blessing. Though far from seeing this journey as I have traced it, the prayer speaks most beautifully of the two termini. It is a greeting of the new moon, which the ancient rabbis considered a symbol of the messianic redemption and renewal of Israel. So highly is this blessing valued that, to one of them, the pronouncing of the words which conclude it: 'Blessed art thou, O Lord, who renewest the months', was like welcoming the divine Indwelling, the Shekinah.

Blessed art thou,
  O Lord our God, King of the universe,
  whose word made the heavens
  and the breath of whose mouth all their host.
Laws and appointed times He gave them
  that they should not falter in their parts.
  Joyfully and glad they are to do the will of their
    Master,
  the true Worker, whose work is truth.
The moon He bade to renew herself,
  a crown of beauty for those He upholds from
    the womb.
  In the time to come they will be renewed like her,
  and will glorify their Maker for the honour of
    His Kingdom.[26]

---

[26] The prayer is a talmudic text, Sanh. 42a. See *The Babylonian Talmud*, ed. I. Epstein (London: Soncino Press, 1935-48), Sanhedrin, I, pp. 271-272; or *The Authorised Daily Prayer Book*, ed. Hertz, p. 995. For further material on the blessing of the new moon, see *The Jewish Encyclopedia*, IX, p. 244.

CHAPTER 2

The Chosen Word

THE incarnate Word of God once said, 'How can you understand my doctrine since you do not understand my language?' The inscribed Word of God could say the same thing. For just as God committed himself to the possibilities and limitations of human flesh, so he commits himself to the possibilities and limitations of the human tongue. Inspiration and Incarnation are two analogous modes of being of the divine Word. And the mode of being is in each case human—more closely to our theme, it is in each case Semitic. To express a revelation which in itself transcends all fashions of human thought, God has chosen one thought-framework: that of the Semitic world. This is the fact, the datum we accept on faith. It could have been otherwise. The time and place of the revelation might have been twentieth-century England: we might have been taught to look forward to the Commonwealth of God, not his Kingdom; we might have expected not a King-Messiah after the manner of David, but a Messiah-Queen after the fashion of Elizabeth. Why the revelation should in fact be made at that place and in that time can only be conjectured. No doubt both time and place were peculiarly apt. I have heard it said that a crucifixion ten years later would have made all the difference. However that may be, it is certain that Alexander and Julius Caesar had paved Christianity's way. And a place midway between New York and Tokyo was indeed a suitable rendezvous for the most diverse of cultures. But this is speculation and we must face the facts: the Bible is alien to us because it is ancient and because it is distant. Its language is archaic and foreign. How can we understand its doctrine?

Now it is not the language barrier, in the narrow

sense of the phrase, that prohibits our understanding of the Bible. A year's study could almost cure that, or the use of a verbatim translation. But it is the *mind* of the Bible that is a world away from our habits of thought. So many biblical troubles come from that. We forget that God has chosen not the philosophy of the West for his vehicle but the wisdom of the Middle East. If this fact with all its implications is sufficiently recognised, a host of difficulties will disappear.

Whether conscious of it or not, we are children of the Greeks.[1] Our profane culture, insofar as it is not complemented by Biblical religious training, is basically Greek. That is to say, it is essentialist: it strives to attain the thing in itself, it asks not what it does but what it is. It is also dualist: that is, it distinguishes the matter from the form which this matter as it were 'takes'. These two qualities are of course interdependent. It is therefore abstract or intellectualist rather than concrete and moral, static rather than dynamic, dualist rather than monistic. Semitic, and specifically biblical thought is existentialist, concerned with the thing as it acts, and monistic—the distinction between matter and form and therefore between matter and spirit is alien to it. There is a roughness about the Hebrew mind that contrasts with the smoothness of the Greek. Perhaps we may compare the Greek mind with a professor lecturing on the Georgics, the Semitic mind with a practical farmer. Or we may oppose the delicate metre of Greek verse with the unmetrical hammered rhythm of Hebrew poetry. Or again, as has been suggested, we may confront the Parthenon with Solomon's Temple: on the one hand elegant proportion and structural logic, on the other a building entirely functional—so many boxes placed side by side. For the Hebrew is practical where the Greek is speculative; accordingly, he will be reluctant to formulate definition. One who asks, 'Who is my neighbour?'

[1] The term 'Greek' is commonly used in this connection, though loosely. In fact, the contrast we describe is not so much with classical Greek philosophical thought as with its more or less distorted, though widely distributed, inheritance.

can expect not a definition but an example of neigh-
bourliness. A Roman who asks, 'What is truth?' may
get no answer, or if an answer is found it will prove to
be an imperative invitation: 'I am the Way, the Truth,
the Life'. And if a man ask, 'How many will be
saved?', the reply will be oblique and practical:
'Strive to enter by the narrow gate'.

Of these two divergent outlooks the products are
numerous; we must be content to indicate only a few.
And first, the notion of God. Greek theological
thought first passed through the stage of myth when
gods were many and cruel and sensual, and finally to
the Aristotelian *Actus Purus,* a God non-spatial, non-
temporal, non-finite, pure Truth, Act, Being—an abstract essence, a pure Idea reached after long 'contem-
plation' from a distance. Old Testament thought on
the other hand starts not so much from a consideration
of natural phenomena as from a sense of the living
Presence, transcendent indeed, but, unlike Aristotle's
supreme principle, intimately interested in the people
he had chosen. And since the Hebrew idea of God—
'consciousness' of God might be a more suitable word
—is derived so largely from Israel's own historical
and providential experience, it is constantly being enriched not by further intellectual examination but by
what may be called an accumulation of intuitions.
If one likes to call this approach a defect,[2] let us at
least acknowledge its corresponding quality. The
cold God of the Greek becomes a strong-handed father, a soft-hearted mother, a bitterly jealous lover.
He is a living God; he is almost too human. Yet the
Bible never falls into the trap of the mythologies; the
God of the Hebrews has no consort, for example.
And indeed, if any religion is to be vital it must of
necessity anthropomorphize: human comparisons,
however inadequate, are indispensable and we daily
accept our own convention; moreover, the anthropo-

---

[2] But in truth we are delivering no comparative value-judg-
ments on the two outlooks we speak of. After all, they are complementary approaches.

morphism of the Old Testament was itself a preparation for accepting the last almost incredible anthropomorphism which we call the Incarnation. At any rate,
the anthropomorphic method safeguards the personality of God, and any pantheistic tendency is firmly
excluded.

But if we are still troubled by anthropomorphism
let us return to the principle we have declared, namely that the Hebrew is not interested in essential definition and there is no attempt at a definition of God
here. It is rather that the Semite is saying, 'He *acts*
like a father', 'He *acts* like a mother'. In other words,
the Hebrew's theology is functional. Therefore it
could be misleading, for instance, to ask what the
Hebrews thought the false gods *were*. The question
might seem sufficiently simple, but its answer must
take account of the dynamic content of the Hebrew
verb 'to be' which includes 'to become' and 'to effect'.
Perhaps we should ask rather what the Hebrews
thought the false gods could do—and the answer is
'nothing, compared with what the God of Israel could
do'. Similarly, when the fool says in his heart 'there
is no God', he is not denying God's existence but the
intervention of his avenging providence (cf. Ps 10:4;
Hebr.). And when a Hebrew thinks of his God as the
one who 'is', here too the verb is pregnant with the
idea of effectiveness and power. We may add that his
'definition' of Man also is in terms of his function.
The first chapter of Genesis places Man in a hierarchy
of dominion: his likeness to God lies precisely in his
domination of the beasts and by this domination he is
distinguished from them: there is no attempt at a
'definition' of their respective 'natures'.

As for the 'knowledge' man has of God, here too
we must take account of the Hebrew thought-world.
It is not without significance that the Hebrew thinks
'in his heart', while the viscera are the seat of emotion.
He moves our own imagery down by one storey. Our
verb 'to know', since we use it in a context which we
call 'Greek', is by no means the exact equivalent of
the Hebrew verb we use it to translate. It is sad that

we have no adequate equivalent whatever, and this is
an illustration of the impossibility of translation from
one culture to another. 'He knew her not' (we translate) 'till she brought forth her son'; or 'This is eternal
life: that they should know thee the one true God';
'My people is made captive because they have not
known the Lord'; the sons of Heli are wicked, they do
not 'know' the Lord. It is evident from these and a
thousand examples that 'knowledge' is no abstract
thing here but a personal experience and action accordingly; engagement of heart, as we should say, as
well as of head. It follows immediately from this
that the verb 'to believe' is not abstract either. It pre-
sumes of course that the object of 'belief' is there, but
it implies much more than asserting that it is there—
it implies a personal commitment to it. Here is all the
difference between 'I believe *in* God' and 'I believe
that there is a God'.

Of that other activity of the mind that we call 'memory' something similar may be said. For us, 'to remember' is to carry ourselves backwards in time to
the event's occurrence. In biblical thought, to 'remember' is rather to call the past event into the present and make it active there. Thus in the moment
when God 'remembers' a sin, that sin begins to make
itself felt, to work its deadly effects. With this in mind
we may read with new eyes the formula: 'Do this in
remembrance of me'. The ritual of 'commemoration'
now brings the crucified Christ from the past into the
present.[3]

We observe a similar dynamism in the verb 'to
speak'. In Hebrew, *dabar* means not only 'word', but
'deed' or 'thing'. Thus in Luke's Infancy Narrative,
which has a Hebrew or Aramaic substratum, the shep-
herds say, 'Let us go over to Bethlehem and see this
word (i.e., thing) that has come to pass'. This refusal
to make up a sharp distinction between 'word' and
'deed' prepares us for the Hebrew idea that a thing

---

[3] Cf. N. Clark, *An Approach to the Theology of the Sacraments*, (London, 1956), p. 62.

speaks and a word acts. An important conclusion
follows. The God-guided events of Israel's history
are words of God, revelations. To confuse biblical
revelation with, or rather to restrict it to the 'so says
the Lord' would be to mistake this central fact. History is prophecy in the correct sense of the word—it is
the voice of God admonishing. This is to say that all
history is God's word and therefore under his dominion, from which neither crime nor sin is subtracted.
It is a corollary of this, and equally typical of the
Hebrew mentality as we have described it, that no
distinction is made between what we call the absolute
and the permissive will of God. It is not simply that
if a woman is barren it is God who closes the womb,
but that if Pharaoh is stubborn it is God who hardens
his heart, and if an evil spirit comes upon Saul it is
'from the Lord'. It is true that from many another
text we know that human responsibility remains, but
the problem is not resolved in biblical thought—unless it is finally the practical solution reached by the
prophets, which after all is the only useful solution to
a problem that is still mysterious, namely the achievement of the peak of man's freedom in a surrender to
God's dominion.

What we have said of God's self-revelation, his
'word', by means of history, may help us to solve a
serious difficulty, serious because it arises in the realm
of theology which is precisely the Bible's business.
There are not a few moral shortcomings narrated
without reproval, even with tacit approval, by the
biblical writers. Abraham's deceit of the Pharaoh,
for instance; Jacob's fraud of Esau; the cruelty of the
herem or sacred massacre—said to be commanded
by God moreover; the occasional bloodthirsty prayers
of the Psalms; polygamy; divorce; legitimized rape
in warfare. It is not enough to answer that much of
this was the commonplace of contemporary war, that
much is exaggerated in books written long after the
events, that the acts of a nation were at that time always attributed to its god, that God has universal
rights over human lives, and so on. We must go back,

it seems, to what we have said about the Hebrew's knowledge of God having been conveyed to him by history—a consequence, we may remember, of his pragmatic outlook. The immediate consequence of this—as it would not have been if Israel had had an Aquinas inspired by God in his metaphysical researches—is that the knowledge slowly progresses as history slowly progresses. Now development means progress from *imperfection*. And it is to be remembered that in the Old Testament there is real progress, real addition to knowledge, not merely development or explicitation of knowledge already implicitly possessed. Now this knowledge, as we have seen, is primarily practical: it is a knowledge of the living, interested, demanding God; it has man's response to God's offer to man for its focus of attention. In other words, Israel was being educated by providential history in a course of *moral* monotheism. She was making toward a more perfect morality—which means that the previous morality was less perfect. If we keep this in mind, we shall avoid mental acrobatics as unworthy of ourselves as they are repulsive to others, by which we may attempt to justify the unjustifiable simply because it is biblical.

If this irks us from the theological point of view, so much the worse for our theological point of view which, ultimately, is thus demonstrated to be anti-Incarnationist. In the name of a false theology we are being revolted by the soundest and the most mysterious datum of the Christian creed—that God does his work through man, through man with all his imperfections. It is no new theological idea (Chrysostom for one was at home with it) this condescendance of God to the level of man, to the moral sense of a chosen people, a people chosen not for its virtue, as the prophets abundantly assure us, but for some reason known only to God. From this flows the most pervasive and the most helpful of all principles of biblical interpretation—as indeed it is of all rational secular interpretation—namely that before we judge we must read through to the end. Only the doctrine of Christ himself, by proposing the highest, will show what depths lie behind, and yet how God's people were slowly climbing out of them.

We have now discussed some of the consequences of the Semitic outlook from an interpretational, almost an apologetic, point of view; but there is one result of it which might be particularly stressed because its roots are thrust through the whole of the Bible. It is an idea that must be grasped if we are to understand the Pauline doctrine of the Church and, perhaps unexpectedly, to find a solution in principle for the ills of our own time. In case our aim should at this point seem obscure, let us consider a parable composed by a Jewish rabbi in about 150 A.D. A number of men, he said, were in a boat. One of them took out an awl and began to drill a hole in the boards where he sat. When his companions objected he replied, 'What are you worrying about? I am only drilling a hole in my part of the boat.' The lesson is obvious: *esprit de corps,* community spirit. Towards this, and much more, we shall be working in what follows.

Of the Semitic mind we used the term 'monistic', as opposed to the Greek tendency to dualism. The Greeks asked themselves certain questions, unimagined by the Hebrews, which led them to distinguish form from matter, soul from body, so that their conception of man has been said—somewhat unfairly— to be that of an angel in a slot-machine, soul imprisoned in flesh. It was otherwise with the Hebrew. He made no sharp distinction between soul and body: man does not have a body, he is a body; he is an animated body, not an incarnate soul. For the Hebrew there is no dead body but dust.[4] From this un-Greek conception it follows that the whole man is engaged before God: it is not just a soul that aspires to God. We can readily see how sound a morality this may lead to in the end, how no withdrawal from the body can

[4] On all this cf. the excellent Pauline study by J. A. T. Robinson, *The Body* (London, 1952).

satisfy biblical religion, though it may involve somewhat strange ideas about bodily purity in the beginning. Now the same refusal to make sharp distinctions
led to another important result. The Greek had two
terms for 'body': the *sarx* (flesh) which man had in
common with his fellows, and the *soma* (body) which
distinguished him from others and made him an individual. But the Hebrew did not thus distinguish *soma*
from *sarx*: he had only one word for 'body'. It is
evident therefore that he had no way of marking one
man off clearly from his fellows—evidently he did not
see the need to do so. Now this is interesting. From
other indications we know of the Hebrew idea of corporate personality: how the clan or tribe or race
might corporately enjoy the name of its individual
patriarch—'Israel' itself is the name of one of Jacob's
sons — and how the importance of circumcision
springs from the fact that it is a badge of nationhood,
an incorporation into a people chosen. This is not to
say that man was not individuated at all, that there is
no interest in the individual, but that he was not individuated by the body as such. He was most certainly
an individual, but an individual in virtue of his relationship as an individual with God—what has been
called a vertical relationship.

This should help us to see how it is that the Bible
is the book of the little man, and of man in society.
The Greek ideal of heroism, the bold and lonely seeking after individual perfection, is not the ideal of the
Bible. To begin with, the power in Samson's hair is
related to God, is God's power; the power in David's
sling is God's power. This means that the first condition of effective heroism is abandonment; its second
condition is that it is not individual but within and for
the community. Now here is where the Bible is so
modern. Men are increasingly aware that the old selfish individualism must go and attempts are being
made all over the world at government level to exor-
cize it. There is danger here as well as hope, danger
that man may lose his individuality altogether, that
we may see only one half of the biblical vision. The

only way to fend off this very real peril is to think wholly biblically; to preserve the one true axis of man's personality which is his individual, 'vertical', relationship with God. This is just another way of stating the old formula that the brotherhood of man is impossible without the fatherhood of God.

We have tried to show that biblical thought does not come naturally to us. It may be, therefore, that we have faults to find with the Bible because we are looking for the wrong things in it and for the wrong mentality behind it. We should remember that truth, though absolute, may be approached in different ways and that the 'Greek' way is not the only way nor even necessarily the best way. It would be foolish to suggest that we should throw overboard the great intellectual legacy of Greece—indeed the Church herself has entered into it with her formulations: thus the terms 'nature' and 'person' for example are unbiblical and Greek; but we must carry this cargo on one side of the ship and the Semitic cargo on the other. The two approaches are complementary. Let us remember at least that if we think our theology in Greek fashion and in the formulae of the Greeks, it should never be without reference to the Semitic mind which, after all, God chose for the medium of his revelation. So for example we may and must think of our Lord as the 'second person' of the blessed Trinity, but we should also think of him, in the biblical phrase, as the Word of God — still remembering that the Semitic 'word' is not an abstract defining thing but a powerful act, sharp as a two-edged sword.

We must learn, too, that it is not the knowledge of God in the Greek sense that is the beginning of wisdom, but the practical fear of the Lord. That this reverence must be worked out in our bodies, not imagining that in some strange way our bodies may seek one thing and our souls another. That it is not to be worked out by ourselves and for ourselves alone but within and for the great society of the sons of men who are sons of God too, radiating outward to them from the body of Christ which we call the Church.

CHAPTER 3

The Saving Word

WE have seen what an 'effective thing' a 'word' is for the Hebrew. If God utters a word it is not to satisfy idle curiosity but to produce a real effect: the Word is imperative, not indicative merely. And if it is God's word, we may presume that this effect is aimed at man's highest level of thought and activity. This is to say that the Bible is and must be theology. 'The Bible is history' is the meanest of compliments. No doubt 'The Bible: History or Theology?' is a crude alternative, and a misleading one as we shall shortly explain, but it is as well to put the question if only to uncover a hidden fault. For years we have been plagued with a subject so ominously and so danger-ously called 'Bible History', a subject from which we carried away so many strange stories and so few profound ideas.

But to prevent later misunderstandings, we should make it plain at the outset that we are not denying, we are very far from denying, the historical element in Old Testament and New. For if anything is clear from the reading of the Bible it is that the sacred authors were convinced that God had intervened in the history of the old Israel and of the new: he had intervened notably to produce a marvellous exodus, first from Egypt, second from a tomb. These are what we call historical facts. Nevertheless, it is salutary to ask ourselves on what the stress must be laid and the time spent in our study, or teaching, of the Bible. Is it to be on the precise nature of the Egyptian plagues that set Israel free and on the dovetailing of the Gos-pel narratives of the Resurrection, or is it to be on the redemptive nature and consequences of the Egyp-tian exodus and on the redemptive nature and conse-quences of the Resurrection in virtue of which our

own bodies are redeemed and glorified? If it is re-
torted that this is a matter of emphasis only, it might
fairly be replied that emphasis may be all important.

In the biblical perspective history is alive with God.
The polytheist and the pantheist are bound up with
the cycle of nature; their hope is born yearly in the
Spring, and it is a hope of earth; when this hope fails
nothing is left. But the Israelite accepted no god
immanent in nature; his was a personal God, the free
and independent maker and controller of nature, a
craggy and stubborn God who would not conform
with nature's cycle. For the Hebrew hope might
bloom in the winter, and when earth's hope failed
he looked instinctively to heaven, because the God of
the Hebrew is the God who interferes. It is the same
with history. This God does not merely use history,
he makes it. That is why he is the God of the two
great historical religions, that is to say of the two
religions that claim divine intervention in history for
their founding: Judaism and Christianity. History is
God in action, and the particular history the Bible
relates is regarded by the Hebrew as God's chosen
sphere of self-revelation, it is his 'word'. The book
of Deuteronomy puts this attitude clearly enough in
contrast with the religions of nature:

When you lift your eyes to the sky and see the sun
and moon and stars and all the array of heaven,
do not be tempted to fall down and serve them.
The Lord your God has given all these things to
every nation under heaven. But as for you, the
Lord has seized you and led you out from Egypt,
the furnace of fire, that you may become the people
of his inheritance.

The Hebrew read the story of his race as an interpretation of God. Delivery, fall, repentance, rescue,
these were Israel's recurring seasons, and in these she
found a God powerful, intolerant, eager, forgiving.
She acknowledged no such agnostic word as 'coinci-
dence', no inevitable fate, no repetitive circles of time.

Quite the opposite: not a sparrow fell without the hand of God, repentance and prayer could move God's heart and turn catastrophe, a Providence drove along rectilinear time to some future goal that was not merely Paradise regained but a new heaven and a new earth.

Israel knew God from historical experience, therefore, and accumulating experience deepened the knowledge. To take but one example, the experience of calamity and exile taught Israel what God expected of her: it taught her that she had a mission in the world, to those who had exiled her and to others, and that this mission was to be exercised by suffering. Thus in the second part of *Isaias* we have a picture of the expected ideal, though the expectation was to be fulfilled in only one of Israel:

> Despised and shunned by men . . . pierced for our sins . . . torn from the land of the living . . . multitudes for his portion.

Now if historical events thus revealed God's purposes, then we may not speak of 'History *or* Theology'. In such a context, history *is* theology, and broadly speaking it is for the sake of its theological lessons that history is used.

For it is worth noting that the Hebrew name for the Old Testament is 'the Law, the Prophets, and the Writings'. What we too readily call the histories the Hebrews group under the 'Later Prophets' or the 'Writings'. The Hebrew did not cultivate history for its own sake. If factual detail appeared to him without significance he might make free with it or ignore it. Whether we like this approach or not is beside the point; it is the Semitic approach, the biblical approach, God's approach. If we look for history in the modern fashion we are looking for something which the inspired author, and therefore God, does not intend to give: history is a plan of God working through historical events, and these events are an outward sign less important than its inward meaning.

The author therefore, whose intention and formal judgment are of the theological order, is liberated from the minutiae of events; his purpose influences the literary form he chooses. Let us take an example. 'In the four hundred and eightieth year after the exodus from Egypt, Solomon built the temple of God.' Is this a formal historical judgment? We must not be hasty, forewarned as we are by our knowledge of the Hebrew mind. First let us consider this other biblical statement: 'From the first temple, of Solomon, to the second temple, of Zorobabel, there were twelve generations of priests'. Now a Hebrew 'generation' being normally reckoned as forty years, we receive the impression that just as the temple of Solomon was 480 years after the exodus, so the temple of Zorobabel was 480 years after Solomon's. Is this fact or artifice? We know that Solomon's temple dates approximately to 960 B.C.; are we to conclude to the following list: Exodus 1440, Solomon's temple 960, Zorobabel's 480? In a modern history book, yes; in biblical writing, no. The author's formal judgment is rather of the theological order: he wishes to place the Solomonic temple exactly midway between the first model of a temple (the Tabernacle of the Exodus period) and the temple of his own time (Zorobabel's) indicating legitimate continuity. One feels that if a further conclusion is possible, it would at least be quite consistent with the author's intention that if a third temple were to be built, this also would come approximately 480 years later still; which was indeed the time when One spoke of the temple of his body, raised up after three days.

If we recognize, therefore, that the operative word of God is concerned with salvation and not with unsalutary information we shall learn to see the Bible in perspective. We shall have no sense of shock if we read that Job or Tobias or Jonas are literary figures only and not historical personages; what should justly shock us would be a denial of the theological significance of these individuals whether fictitious or not. The book of Job, not Job, is the important thing—its theological discussion of the problem of evil, the great moral lessons of Tobias, the wonderful picture of the all-embracing mercy of God in Jonas, all these things matter; the framework of the picture is a literary, but not a historical necessity. We shall not be surprised either if the books of Judith and Esther are what the Jews themselves call 'midrash', edifying stories with an element of fantasy, deliberately contrived with the purpose of inculcating devotion to the Law, to the virtues and the like. There is nothing in the Catholic doctrine of Inspiration that is opposed to these possibilities—and they are possibilities of varying grades. If there is scandal here, it comes from the old term and method of 'Bible History' and not from sound Catholic theology.

It is possible to live in the past, but very dangerous: to think a motor-car a handsom cab could be a mortal miscalculation. It is possible to be preoccupied with out-of-date and superficial objections and to be distracted from the enduring substance. It is possible to be obsessed with the nineteenth century attack on the Bible as a document scientifically untrustworthy. In spite of ourselves a feeling of relief may come when we read that the Bible is as historically reliable as an Assyrian monument. But to put the matter thus is already a useful warning and brings us to our senses. It reminds us that the Bible is first and foremost God's *saving* word, and to this any incidental historical information is subordinated. If we constantly and consciously advert to the fact, so obvious as to pass unnoticed, that the Bible is a tool of God for *salvation,* our interpretation will be healthy and to the point.

Nevertheless, a word, God's word, cannot like water or oil be efficaciously administered to the unconscious. It saves by being known—a statement that may be securely made now that we have explained how 'knowledge' in this context is acceptance and personal commitment. Now the first stage in this process of 'knowledge' is comprehension of the word's meaning in a given setting. The interpreter therefore

cannot ignore background, and the background may
be historical circumstances or literary tradition. Paul's
alarming pronouncement, for example, that he thanks
God he has baptized none of the Corinthians moves
into focus when we learn how rival factions gathered
round the several baptizers, threatening to divide an
allegiance that is Christ's. And as for literary tradition, a disputed sentence like 'Where the body is, there
will the eagles be gathered together' cannot be interpreted without taking account of it: it is at least an
element in the argument that Jeremias should use the
same figure of Jerusalem destroyed and picked white
by the invader; perhaps we would do better to translate: 'Where the carcass is, there will the vultures be
gathered together'. The one whom the Word would
touch, therefore, cannot be contemptuous of literary
and factual history. For it must never be forgotten
that the written Word was addressed primarily to the
sacred author's contemporaries; we are looking over
their shoulders; it is taken from their vocabulary,
which we must take the trouble to consult. It may
even be (we may remark in passing) that the Word,
yes even the word of God, has no *immediate* saving
power for us. To take an example, the name-lists in
the book of Esdras leave us unmoved. Yet these
served to re-establish the authentic Israel in its land,
and from this authentic Israel came Christ, the saviour of us all. This particular Word, therefore, has
already done its saving work and for us it has no more
to do.

This should draw our attention to the necessity of
watching the Word as it grows. It is understandable
that this procedure has been so often neglected. Exact
dating of biblical books and parts of books is frequently very difficult, and the biblicist has often been
a poor theologian, the theologian an indifferent biblicist. Nevertheless, approximate dating is usually
sufficient and a measure of agreement is now being
reached; moreover, the end of the temporary, unnatural divorce between biblicist and theologian is already in sight. The issue of the happy reunion will

be a theology, dogmatic and moral, that is seen to be
alive, known as only a mother can know her child because she has watched every stage of his development.
We may take one simple and pervasive example: the
interesting and consoling process by which the vague
question-mark of suffering straightens into its answer,
the Cross.

The Bible is not a restful book; on the contrary, it
is disturbing. It seeks no escape from reality but confronts it and worries over it. Nor does it offer a recipe
for a peace of mind that is to be pursued, however
harshly, in the isolated self. It permits us to see even
from the beginning that peace is not an achievement
but a gift. We already know, before the question of
suffering is explicitly put—and it was a long time before Israel put it clearly—that no solution is possible
within a closed human system. 'Seek *me*', says Amos,
the earliest of the prophets, 'and you shall live'.
Peace, if there is to be peace, comfort, if there is to
be surcease from suffering, is only from God. But
Israel's acute sense of national solidarity ensured that
the question of suffering should first be posed at the
national level. A rough answer seemed to be at hand:
national betrayal of God brings national disaster from
God, national repentance brings national recovery.
This is the underlying thesis of the book of Judges.
This neat equation was used at first, somewhat naïvely,
to formulate individual experience, and so the tran-
quil sentence could be written in Israel: 'I was young
and have grown old and never seen a just man want-
ing for bread'. Suffering was through man's own
fault, or at least that of his people: 'Has this man
sinned or his parents?' is the only solution that occurs
to the unsophisticated when a man is born blind. But
the book of Job—and perhaps we are now as late as
the mid-fifth century — faces the problem squarely.
Here is no facile solution. It is the function of Job
to stand as an example of the man who is irreproach-
able and yet in agony, a challenge to the old groping
solution that virtue is its own reward. Job is a relent-
less book, and it has the courage to end on a note of

interrogation. Yet though theoretical judgment is suspended, indeed almost because it is suspended, there
is advance: there is no answer but in God. Nor is the
practical judgment entirely negative: not resignation
but abandonment is demanded, a generous self-com-
mitment to God's mysteriousness. We should find it
easy to sympathize with this stage of biblical thought:
we find it hard enough ourselves to see suffering not
as a negative infliction but as a positive privilege. But
Job's is not the last word. About a century later (if
the Servant Songs of the book of Isaias are to be put
in the middle of the fourth century) a long step forward is taken. In the description of the Suffering
Servant we recognize the advance Israel has made, or
at least one inspired genius in Israel: suffering may
be strangely productive, it may be the willingly paid
price of our peace; through bruises we may be healed.
The question 'How can the just man suffer?' is re-
torted: 'How can the just fail to suffer?'. The saving
Word is thus gradually shown to be a word of salutary
suffering, not however because it is endured but because it is endured for God's cause and is by God
rewarded.

For we have painted a false picture if the Word of
God seems to be a word about man. The Bible is a
word about God. It can see man only in relation to
God, as creature to Creator. And the relation is not,
as it were, static; it is by this or that posture before
God that man may be assessed. Now since the individual is always seen in that relation, the crisis of one
man—like the experience of the whole nation—may
when reflected upon contribute to the pattern of
images that make up our biblical picture of God. Thus
the impatient Job does not learn only that God is in-
scrutable, he learns also that God is active even in
suffering and riddles. Indeed this Semite, refresh-
ingly free of metaphysical refinement, knows his God
as the one who sends the suffering and sets the riddle;
that in this very act God reveals himself as the Mystery in which suffering has some hidden meaning. A
hundred years later Ecclesiastes reflects upon his ex-

perience, which is not of pain but of pleasure. Disillusionment is *his* revelation: Blessed are not the rich. All that remains is to fear God and obey. It may be said that his experience and the lesson he deduces from it are more subtle than Job's: a God is trustworthy whose earthly gifts do not satisfy. It is only a step from here to 'Blessed are the poor' and the promise of the vision of God.

With these two the Word of suffering grows more articulate. Both Job and Ecclesiastes went forward through the dark—but they went forward. The Word advanced not on sunlit peaks of triumphant prophets but in a gloomy valley. The two could not see their way, but in fact they were going to Calvary; they were learning the deepest divine knowledge of all: that pain and problem are part of a crucified and mysterious God. But here we must repeat what cannot be said too often: that each book of the Bible is only a part of the living word of the living God which must not be arrested and challenged at any stage, or God will cry: 'Wait till I finish'. And he has not finished — even yet.

Yes, the Bible is a saving Word because it is about God. But how is he translated into human words? The Scriptures it seems, would suppose that there is in man, made to the image of God, some resonance in sympathy with his maker; that he can be led by mental image, by pictorial representation, inadequate but not invalid. But let the Bible speak with its own unmetaphysical tongue:

Moses said: Please let me see your glory. And God said: I shall parade all my majesty before you and in your presence utter the name 'Yahweh'. I have compassion on whom I will and pity for all I please. And again God said: You cannot see my face because no man can see my face and live. Here is a place near me. Stand upon the rock, and when my glory passes by I shall put you in a cleft of the rock and I shall shelter you with my hand as I pass by. Then I shall take my hand away and you will see

me from the back; but my face no man can see.
                                        (Exod. 33:18-23),

We smile at the anthropomorphism as if we were not
guilty ourselves. But consider how it lifts biblical language above all fashions of philosophy and how, with
the wisdom of simplicity, it deliberately refuses to
seek entrance into the mystery. And yet it has a deep
significance for its own time. If the Hebrew knew that
no image could be made of his God, he also knew that
God could not be adequately symbolized by sun or
moon or planet. For him the only image possible was
that of a person. The only language by which his
God might be addressed is drawn from the institutions of human society—as Lord, King, Father, Judge
and the like. Anthropomorphism is not the pathetic
childishness we think: it indicates God's personal relation to history, to man's story; as such it is not a
weakness at all—except the weakness of all theological language—but an important witness, not indeed
to what God is but to what God does. And if in the
end what God does is to assume a human nature, why
then we have anthropomorphism in real earnest.

But this Word of God which is a word about God
is no idle self-expression—it is aimed at man's heart,
an invitation that cannot be met with silence but must
be accepted or refused; he who is not for it is against
it. It is a revelation so tender that indifference is a
slap in the face. The Word almost stammers with
anxiety and its expressions are multiple, disconnected,
almost incompatible. God is a father, that and much
more; but he is a mother too, who carries Israel at
the breast. He is Love without qualification, or better—because the Semite true to his genius always
prefers verb to noun—he is loving, in all our imagin-
able ways and beyond them. Let us take the boldest
image of all. Driven almost to incoherence by the
effort to express the ineffable, driven anyway to in-
tolerable daring, the Scriptural writers, both early
and late, preach the *jealousy* of God. God indignantly
insists that he alone is God, that he alone has a just

claim to Israel's affection and appeals for proof to his action in her history: in front of Israel he challenges the gods:

> I am the king and redeemer of Israel,
> I am the first and the last.
> You are my witnesses:
> Is there any other god but me?   (cf. Is 44:6, 8)

But there is worse, or better, than this: God's jealousy is that of a thwarted husband, a figure of ridicule who waits until her lovers tire of his wife:

> She will chase after her lovers and not catch up
>   with them;
> She will seek and not find them.
> Then she will say: I will go back to my first hus-
>   band for I was happier then than now.
>
> (Os 2:9).

God waiting for spoiled goods! It reminds us that the Prodigal found an eager father, though driven home not by love but by starvation. The allegory of Israel, the faithless wife, is recurring reality in her story, and the recurring news about God was that he had been mocked again. It is still the same news, the good news, the gospel. For love of men God came among men and was hanged for it. But the folly of the cross is the best news we ever heard.

You may have noticed that whether we spoke of the Bible's simple anthropomorphism, or of God's foolish love, or of man's senseless suffering, we were drawn relentlessly towards the final revelation in Christ. The taking of a human nature by God—and this is an object of faith—sanctions our thinking of him in terms of man and justifies our language. That same singular event turns figure to fact — or rather shows how fact always lurked behind the figure: man and God are two in one flesh. The death of that flesh and its resurrection show how even suffering, especially suffering, can be used redemptively. And all this is as it should be, for the saving Word made flesh is the climax of God's effort to make his word understood. It is *the* revelation of God to human nature through one human nature, and insofar as the revelation can be put into human words it is Christ who will do it.

But we have said that for the Hebrew the term 'word' signifies not something merely denominative and abstract but something operative, efficient. God's events speak; these are God's words—and the coming of our Lord is no exception. For this coming is itself a world-event of God, culmination of so many. And yet it is unique: unique because this time 'it is not the historical event that becomes a word: the Word itself becomes an historical event.' Christ being what he was, did indeed work our salvation in action and passion; but he also enacted a parable of divine love such as the world had not heard nor would hear again —for he was the Word of God. In the dunghill of this creation, in its sordid history, in its stammering tongue, in its crucified flesh, the truth of God was found. And the last word was the foolish word of the Cross.

CHAPTER 4

The Choosing Word

WHEN we read we surrender for a time, we yield our book the initiative. But the surrender is not unconditional: we reserve the right to criticize and to reject. With the Bible the case is otherwise. The act of faith we make in its divine authorship does not indeed dismiss textural or literary criticism, but this exacting work once done there is no choice but surrender, lasting and absolute. For no sound theology, and certainly no biblical theology, can question that the initiative lies always with God. In the beginning is the Word. To define religion as man's search for God is not satisfactory. Religion is God's search for man, a search for man's heart. We cannot know all the devices God uses to this end, but the Bible is one of them.

By these considerations the Christian's attitude to the Scripture is determined. He does not go to the Bible as to a source-book of facts—even of theological facts. He resists the temptation to equip himself for a biblical 'quiz'. For him the Bible is in all but technical terms a sacrament. He yields to the initiative of the Word, being himself concerned only with removing obstacles to it—an operation which is itself God-furthered. Human scholarship is indeed his eyeglass but he remembers that the purpose of his reading is that he may find himself 'apt and well equipped for every good work'. The purpose but not the ultimate purpose, because the work he is now equipped for is to the glory of God. So the heaven-earth-heaven parabola of the Word is finished: God's word does not return to him void.

But the Word initiates in history too: it sets in motion the machinery of God's plan for mankind and directs it through every crisis. It alights where it will,

disconcertingly perhaps: in Haran, on Sion, in Babylon itself. It chooses the ground in which it will take
root, and the human group through which its saving
work is to be done. But it is important at this stage
to ask what such a choice does not imply. When we
speak of a 'chosen race' we do not mean that each
single member of that race, precisely as an individual,
is the recipient of God's particular favour. We must
distinguish clearly between God's collective election
and his dealings with the individual who belongs to
that chosen body of men. Doubtless the individual of
the group would be aware of religion's truths and the
demands of morality more than those outside it, but
whether in the *qahal* of the Old Testament or the
ekklesia of the New he has to acquit himself personally before God—only God knows how well or how
ill. The choice we are speaking of is no canonization
of the individual but the vocation of a group, a grace
generously bestowed (*gratis data*) but not itself sanc-
tifying (*gratum faciens*). But in virtue of this choice
Israel became irrevocably the instrument of the Word;
henceforth 'salvation is of the Jews'. In this sense
God 'loves Jacob and hates Esau'—to effect his purpose he chooses Israel and not the Edomites.

Why God should choose this group rather than that
is scarcely a useful question. St Paul would have
resented it:

Is not the potter master of his clay
to make from the same lump
a vessel for special occasions and a vessel for every-
    day use?

No doubt Israel's geographical and psychological
isolation could be expected to preserve monotheism
from contamination in an idolatrous world, but this
is conjecture. Israel was chosen simply because God
willed to choose her. This is God's own answer and
man must be content with it:

I shall be gracious to whom I will to be gracious:
I shall show mercy to whom I will to show mercy.

Indeed it is even suggested that Israel was chosen because from all human points of view she was the least suitable of all. The book of Deuteronomy says expressly:

> If the Lord chose you,
> it was not because you are the most numerous of peoples;
> rather you are the least.
> It was because of his love for you.

Which is to say, because he willed it. Taking the hint from this text we might venture to say—and there is profound religious truth here — that this choice of Israel was the first example of God's steady policy to choose the weakest so that his own power might show the more. When another divine choice came to be made, this time of the poor and ignorant Corinthians, St Paul comments:

> God has chosen what is weak in this world
> so that no man may boast in the face of God.

But though it is unhelpful, impertinent perhaps, to ask why God should choose Israel rather than any other, it is important to ask what function he had in mind for Israel when he chose her. The answer is of consequence because it is the answer also to the question why he chose us Christians. Now it is evident that God himself must be the goal of all his action, and this truth is precisely that which the biblical doctrine of choice, or 'election', asserts. The object of God's choice of Israel is the glory, that is to say the public proclamation, of God's name — or of God's person, to use our own idiom. Thus Ezechiel preaches:

> I will sanctify my great name;
> and the nations shall know,
> when through you I show my sanctity,
> that I am the Lord.

By its own separateness from the other nations

Israel is to be a witness to God's own unassailable isolation — that is, to his sanctity. In this way the Israelite, like the Christian, is to be in the world, visible to the world, an example to the world, but not of the world. Not that either Israelite or Christian works of his own motive-power; but he is God's weapon.

In particular the marvellous exodus from Egypt will declare God's 'sanctity' which, we repeat, is what we should call his 'transcendence', his majesty beyond the reach of human hostility. So the divine voice in the book of Exodus says:

> I will cover myself with glory
> at the expense of Pharaoh and his army;
> and the Egyptians shall know
> that I am the Lord.

That, then, is the purpose of God's choice—the making known of God's glory; and it is this our Lord bids us pray for when he tells us to say 'hallowed be thy name'. God's purpose throughout Old Testament and New is consistent: and that is why St Paul can say that all these things are written for our correction.

Israel therefore was chosen as 'God's point of attack on the world', and the attack was at its height in the Exodus, so that the book of Deuteronomy can exclaim, looking back on this event which convinced Israel that the hand of God was with her:

> Is there any god
> who has ever set out to seek a nation from all others
> by prodigies and victories and signs—
> all those things you have seen with your own eyes,
> things that the Lord performed in Egypt?

Insistence on this theme is typical of the book of Deuteronomy where we find the classical formulation of the choice:

> You are a people consecrated to the Lord your God.

It is you whom the Lord has chosen
to be his own people
among all the nations that are on earth.

In the same way, the inspired author in the book of
Genesis is equally convinced that the Exodus showed
clearly that God had chosen his people; he therefore
seeks back into the twilight of history for signs of this
choice. His method is one of convergence, or the narrowing-down of perspective to demonstrate the sure
selective process. It is evident that our author wants
us to see how God's promise of hope after the Fall
lies within a certain group of mankind. Of the sons
of Adam he names only three. Abel is murdered and
Cain wanders out of the narrative, leaving us only
with Seth from whom all the antedeluvian patriarchs
descend, until we come to Noah. With Noah comes
the Deluge and the rest of mankind are as it were
washed out of the story.

At this stage a new divine promise is made: the
rainbow Noah sees is a symbol that God has laid aside
his avenging bow—a sign of peace between God and
the remnant of mankind. But again the perspective
is narrowed. Of Cham, Japhet, and Sem, the three
sons of Noah, the author makes it clear that God's
blessing is to go not with Cham, ancestor of the peoples of Asia Minor, nor with Japhet, representing the
peoples of the south—of Egypt and Ethiopia—but
with Sem, father of the Semitic peoples of whom were
the Hebrews and of whom in particular was Abraham.

To Abraham the great promise was made, or renewed, and obedient to God's call he migrated from
Lower Mesopotamia to the land promised him. But
the author of Genesis has not yet sufficiently localized
the group in whom the divine favour lies. He therefore goes on to show how among Abraham's sons it
was not Ismael, father of the Arabs, but Isaac who
was chosen; and of the sons of Isaac not Esau, ancestor of the Edomites, but Jacob whose later name was
Israel. And when Israel's descendants in Egypt after
a time of prosperity came to be persecuted, Moses was

the chosen deliverer. With him the promise was sealed
and signed by covenant; and Israel was formally con-
secrated to God:

> Henceforth if you obey the terms of my covenant,
> I will account you my special possession among the
>   nations,
> and as a kingdom of priests, a nation consecrated.

At this point we should notice the dangers attend-
ing a people who quite rightly believed that they were
the object of God's special choice, dangers to which
many of the Pharisees were to succumb many years
later — I mean the confusion we have already mentioned of divine choice with divine approval. The
peril is considerable when the stress is laid upon the
nation rather than on the individual. This emphasis
is to be observed in the book of Judges for example,
where the fortunes of the nation fluctuate with the
moral conduct of the nation as a whole. The same
emphasis explains a sentence that might perturb the
reader of the Old Testament:

> I am the Lord thy God. . . .
> visiting the iniquity of the fathers upon the children
> unto the third and fourth generation.

For it was true then, as it is now, that a nation as a
whole suffers for denying the law of God—the guilty
with the innocent. The prophets, too, aimed their
attack against a sinful nation as one collectively guilty
thing. The idea of individual sin is of course latent in
all this, but it remains without emphasis. God was
first using the simple and obvious appeal of national
consciousness so that in the course of time he might
bring his people to a concern for individual conscience. But the prophet Jeremias saw the danger in
the sixth century. He announced:

> In those days they shall no longer say:
> 'The fathers have eaten sour grapes
> and the teeth of the children are set on edge'.
> Each man shall die for his own iniquity.

Yet we have to await Ezechiel some forty years later to take up this plaintive proverb, examine it, question it, dilate upon it as his custom is, and to bring to full awareness the principle of individual responsibility—thus making it clear exactly what divine choice did and did not imply.

Now from this time forward we find in the inspired books a growing interest in the conduct of the individual. With this growing sense, there should have been among the people a weakening of national consciousness. God intended that there should be. The way was being prepared for a wider outlook, for the internationalism or catholicism towards which revelation was driving. By this means God's election, God's choice, was being shown to have possibilities beyond national boundaries. There is little doubt that the ordinary Israelite was very slow to perceive this, but the inspired prophets were not. Already in the eighth century Isaias was speaking of a future temple to which the Gentiles would come; a century or two later Jeremias foretold a new covenant tied to no national Law. But the revelation had still some distance to cover. Even Isaias spoke in terms of Mount Sion, and Jeremias in terms of a Levitical priesthood. Moreover, neither was concerned with practical politics—and it was just on this plane that the tension between nationalism and internationalism was truly felt. We find it in the little community back from exile at the end of the sixth century and after. Thus Esdras insisted that foreigners be expelled, yet he admitted alien proselytes into the community. Malachy, an equally bitter opponent of mixed marriage, nevertheless foretold a sacrifice offered from east to west in an age when God's name would be great among the Gentiles.

It was at this crisis of Israel's thought that the remarkable book of Jonas intervened. It ridiculed the idea that the God of Israel could have no concern for the pagan nations, that God's choice of Israel implied that he despaired of everyone else. In effect the satirical author was doing no more than drawing the conclusion from Israel's age-old revealed doctrine of a universal and merciful God, but his pointed and almost defiant tale of God's favour to Nineveh at the expense of an Israelitic prophet throws his weight decidedly on the side of universalism.

Unhappily this was a losing cause. The dispersal of Israel throughout the world four or three hundred years before Christ and onwards produced a defensive spirit, as we might fear, a closing-in for protection, a renewed national self-consciousness, a stiffening in its confidence of choice. Israel hugged the idea of election to her breast. The persistence and intensification of this mood into Christian times was a great misfortune. That it did persist and increase is witnessed by the treatment of St Paul when he announced that God had called him to the Gentiles: 'Away with such a man from the earth', they cried, 'for it is not fit that he should live'. Though the book of Jonas should have braced Israel for the shock, the notion that the divine choice might eventually embrace all nations proved too much for Israel.

We see now perhaps why it was that our Lord himself, so thoughtful for human failings, said that he was sent only to the lost sheep of the house of Israel, and why he appears never to have gone really beyond the borders where a considerable Jewish population was to be found. Yet he made it clear that he had a place in his heart for the hated Samaritans, that he could and did threaten Israel herself with rejection, that many would come from east and west whereas the sons of the Kingdom, the Israelites themselves, might be cast out. Like his forerunner the Baptist, our Lord knew that God could choose to raise up children to Abraham, children of the election, from the very stones.

But faced with this situation we might begin to ask: What has become of the Choice? After all, choice implies selection of one at the expense of others, and if a privilege becomes universal as it seems now to be, it is no longer a choice. Has Israel lost its privilege? Or in St Paul's words: 'Has God cast away his people?' The apostle answers his own question with a firm 'No'. It is a surprising answer from the apostle of the Gentiles, but he proves it by appealing to the ancient biblical doctrine of the Remnant, the Chosen Few, a doctrine deeply rooted in the earliest traditions of Israel and recurrent in the Prophets. These prophets were not unrealistic optimists. They were convinced of course that God had chosen Israel, but they were only too familiar with the unworthiness of their compatriots. Of these two very different parents, the glorious theological certainty and the sad fact of human experience, was born the notion of the Remnant, the *she'ar* or *peletah* of Israel. The word basically means that section of the nation which survives after disaster; but since Israel's disasters were varied and many, the word takes on varying shades of colour in the course of history. It also narrows down numerically, and we find ourselves in the presence of the similar phenomenon of contracting perspective that we have already noticed in the book of Genesis—it is indeed a continuation of that process.

Before the Babylonian exile in the sixth century the word Remnant is used of those left in Palestine by the conquerors; the hope and the choice of Israel naturally remained in and upon them. During the exile the word indicates those who will return to form the nucleus of a restored nation. After the exile the small community under the spiritual leadership of Esdras is conscious that it constitutes this guaranteed Remnant. But at the same time—and here is a momentous development—it becomes clear that membership is not automatic, it is a moral issue; the Remnant is spared because it has been converted, it inherits the Choice because it is holy. This idea was not new. Two hundred years earlier the prophet Isaias had said the same:

The remnant of Sion
and what is left in Jerusalem
shall be called holy.

But what has happened is that the idea has penetrated to the people. Those who returned were largely those who had profited spiritually from the sad experience of exile; they had held on throughout to their conviction of God's loyalty to his Choice. This conviction drove them to return to the hard conditions of the deserted Holy Land when others had stayed in Babylon with the comfort they had won for themselves.

How did this Remnant fare? Quietly and prosperously enough under the tolerant Persian and later under the Egypt of the Ptolemies. But Seleucid Syria was another matter. Worthiness of the Choice was now indeed to be hardly won. Yet from the persecution there emerged those who refused to compromise with hellenistic liberal ideas, and Judaism could boast of men like the seven martyred brothers who died for the ancient faith. Here was the Remnant, reduced but valiant. As with Christianity, the blood of persecution was a seed and the harvest was rich. It ripened into the piety of many such Jewish homes as prepared Mary herself. There were others too, on this threshold of the Gospel, who were quite explicitly conscious of belonging to the Remnant. In the Essene Document of Damascus, for example, we read:

> The prophet says: 'Strike the shepherd and the flock will be dispersed; but I will stretch out my hand to the little ones! . . . Those who remain faithful to him are the poor ones of the flock. These shall be saved in the time of visitation.'

This confidence of being chosen could degenerate —as in the worst of Pharisaism—but it was safe when it was without presumption. Thus the community of Qumran, itself an Essene group, did well to make it expressly their first purpose 'to seek God', to declare itself a home for penitents, to make 'truth, humility, love of goodness, mercy' the most common words of their vocabulary.

It will be seen therefore, at this period of Israel's development, that the emphasis has moved to the individual though the traditional doctrine of collective choice has not been deserted. Each must surrender to the Choice if he is to qualify as a member of the Remnant. This surrender in its most perfect form is portrayed in the post-exilic picture of the ideal servant of God in the second half of the book of Isaias. 'My servant, my chosen one' sanctifies God's name among the nations, and through suffering and even death reconciles the world to the God of Israel. With this portrait we reach 'the high-water mark of all the religious thought of the Old Testament'. We have also come to the last point of the narrowing-down of the chosen Remnant in this chosen One. It is possible, of course, that the inspired poet is thinking of the Remnant itself at its ideal best, but the ideal is so high and the individual note so loud that one is tempted to believe that the poet himself realizes how such a response to divine choice would be rare and even singular. And so in fact it was. Only one Israelite of all the Remnant accepted the office of this Servant of God.

To speak purely theoretically—if this is not waste of time—it might have been otherwise. The twelve apostles at least might have died with him and not deserted him. He might have been crucified not between two thieves but between James and John who had said they could drink of his chalice. But he died alone, the remnant of the Remnant, the chosen *one* of God. Perhaps this is what makes St Paul use that curious rabbinic argument in his Epistle to the Galatians:

> The promise was made to Abraham and his seed.
> Scripture does not say 'and to his seeds'
> as if speaking of several;
> it indicates only one: 'and to his seed',
> that is to say, Christ.

The promise and the choice, disappointed elsewhere, now dwell in him alone.

And yet not alone. Before he died, our Lord said:

> Unless the grain of wheat
> falls into the ground and dies,
> it remains alone.
> But if it dies,
> it brings forth much fruit.

And so it did. Within three days the spirit of the apostles had rallied again, the first harvest of the seed, the new Remnant of Israel. And within fifty days at the feast of the wheat-harvest which we call Pentecost, at least three thousand Jews had acknowledged Jesus as Messiah. St Paul eagerly accepts this as evidence that God's choice has not gone astray:

> God has not rejected his people whom he foreknew:
> even at this present time there is a remnant chosen
>   by grace.
> Israel failed to obtain what she sought,
> but the remnant have obtained it.

But he cannot believe that these few thousands are sufficient vindication of the promise, and so he makes a prohpecy. He tells his readers that Israel's loss has been the Gentiles' gain; but he warns the Gentiles that there is more to come. When their time (that is to say our time) is full and grace has reached its measure, then another age will dawn — the age of Israel returned.

> As regards the gospel, they are enemies of God for
>   your sake;
> but as regards the election they are beloved
> for the sake of their forefathers.
> For the gifts and call of God are irrevocable.
> Just as you were once disobedient to God,
> but now have received mercy because of their dis-
>   obedience,
> so now they have been disobedient
> in order that by the mercy shown to you
> they also may receive mercy.

And as Paul's mind dwells on the wonder of this great vision of sacred history—of a divine choice accepted by a nation, later rejected by all but a few but persisting in spite of this rejection, and finally laying hold of the whole race once more — he bursts into a cry of astonished joy:

Oh the depths of the riches of the wisdom
and of the knowledge of God!
How unsearchable are his judgments!

Looking back over this long history, the symbolic figure we should now have before our mind's eye is that of a great letter X. This figure represents the progress of the divine choice. At the topmost, widest, part we have the promise made after the Fall that through the descendants of the woman the Fall will be reversed. The narrowing of the top half of the letter symbolizes the progress from mankind in general to Seth, Noah, Sem, Abraham, Jacob (or 'Israel') and to Israel's reduced Remnant. The lower half of our symbol figures the widening-out of the Choice to the twelve chosen apostles, to the few thousand Jews of Pentecost and after, then to the multitude of the Gentiles, and finally to these augmented by the return of Israel herself—which is yet to come.

But the point of intersection where the Choice threatened to go into extinction—that point is Christ, second Adam, Son of Man, head of the body which is the Church. From his time onwards who said: 'Go and make disciples of all nations' and 'take up your cross and follow me', many have come and will come to share in his sufferings; they 'supply what is lacking' in them, not because they are defective but because this Chosen One, this Chosen Remnant, must ultimately be identified in many.

CHAPTER 5

The Constant Word (1)

THERE was a Christian genius of the second century whose name was Marcion. The success of his doctrines, which was deep and wide, suggests that he had something to offer of profound and widespread appeal. And indeed he had: the infinite saving mercy of God is the most moving of themes. Yet this, it appears, he made the parent of a doctrinal system unacceptable to the *grande Eglise* and plainly at variance with her apostolic tradition. For it was impossible, Marcion said, to reconcile the tender fatherhood of Christianity's God with the savage justice of Israel's implacable deity. The Old Testament contradicts the New; the régime of Law and the régime of Grace are incompatible and cannot issue from the same God; the Old Testament must go. Against this caricature the orthodox Church rose as one man, from Gaul to Asia Minor, if we are to judge by the famous names among Marcion's adversaries. This was not surprising. However the harmony of Old Testament and New is to be established—and the problem is not a simple one—the earliest Christians, embracing the outlook of their Master, had no suspicion of the only 'Scripture' they yet knew. On the contrary, it was their sacred credentials: they themselves were the 'new Israel', Jesus was the son of David, the ancient Writings provided their theological vocabulary and the framework of their religious and moral thinking. And the caricature denounced itself also. Marcion had put his case very strongly in the work he called, naturally, 'Antitheses'. Being, like many an enthusiast, an artist in black and white and impatient of pastel shades, he was compelled to brighten the shadows in the New Testament and darken the gleams in the Old. This was done by a ruthless manipulation of the evidence, and Marcion's New Testament was composed only of an expurgated edition of the third gospel with ten of the Pauline epistles: his powerful religious intuition, admirable in itself, had defied the data of apostolic tradition.

But Marcion is dead; can he come out of his grave? He is not, he can, he does. His arguments are with us to-day. The antithesis he claimed to demonstrate is objected still. On the one hand Israel sees in the Cross the contradiction of the Law; on the other, the liberal Gentile might tolerate or ignore the Cross but will have none of the primitive savagery of Israel's God. To do something towards helping the removal of these misconceptions we propose first to recall St Paul's solution of Israel's (and his own) problems; secondly, to remind those who see the Old Testament God only as a God of Wrath that he is in truth a God of Love. We wish to show that the Word of God does not blow hot and cold, that the same Word runs through Old Testament to New.

I. THE LAW AND THE CROSS [1]

A Jewish friend once told me that he had three objections to the Christian position: in the first place the Christian is a polytheist; in the second, he is so obsessed by the hope of a future life that he has no enthusiasm for social justice in this one; thirdly, to found a religion on vicarious suffering is repugnant. For some contribution towards the first difficulty one may be allowed to refer to our first chapter where an approach is made to our Lord's divinity in Old Testament terms. The second objection is matter for the social historian and, without doubt, for examination of conscience. The third is the subject of what follows. We hope to show that the notion of one suffering for others is not in fact alien to the mind of Israel herself and that a vicarious suffering and death can be integrated into the whole historical context of the Law.

[1] The interpretation underlying this presentation is based on that set forth in a profound article by Père Benoit, O.P., in *Revue Biblique*, 1938, pp. 481-509.

Indeed we might go further and say that a vicarious death was demanded by the Law, if once we remember that the Law no less than the Promises was the authentic word of a God just and merciful also.

The idea of vicarious suffering was not foreign to Judaism at the beginning of our era. The stories of Abraham and of Moses had taught Israel at least that the intercession of the just man is powerful with God, and from the book of Job she knew that suffering is not always a punishment — it may be a productive trial. This was appreciated by the great martyred rabbi Aqiba. Judaism knew further that the merits of suffering could, like intercession, be put at the disposal of others. The just man suffering could merit for all the nation and expiate its faults. The doctrine is admirably expressed by the seventh of the brave martyr brothers whom we call the Maccabees:

> I am prepared like my brothers to give my body and life for our fathers' laws, beseeching God to show his favour to the nation. . . . May the wrath of the Almighty, justly fallen upon all our race, fall on my brothers and on me, there to end.

We find the same thought in the saying attributed to Rabbi Yohanan. To him it was objected that leprosy could in no way be regarded as a sign of God's love. He answered: 'A man on whom is found one of the four signs of leprosy is a veritable altar of propitiation.' If this was true of a poor leper, that his sufferings could reconcile sinners to God, what of the great saints of Israel? The *midrash* on the Canticle (1:14) identifies the henna-blossoms by a play of words with 'expiation': 'What is the henna? It is the one who expiates for the sins of Israel' — as the Fathers had done. And this was how the ancient Jewish tradition regarded the patiently borne sufferings of the rabbi Juda the Holy: during all this time, it was said, no beast of burden died in Palestine and this was due to the merits of the saintly rabbi.

One must however, be careful to note that no ancient Jewish text ever attributed to the expected Messiah an expiatory *death,* though in certain circles it was admitted that the Messiah's sufferings would contribute to the sum of merits of the Fathers, thus to appease the divine anger. It was in fact impossible for Judaism, given the primacy of the Law in laying down the rules of expiation, to envisage an expiatory death outside the legal prescriptions—even expiation by suffering seems to have been a concession, a concession possibly made under Christian influence. That the Messiah should die after a reign of glory was certainly admitted; but that his death should be precisely his mission was inconsistent with the perpetuity of the Law, with the honour of the Messiah himself, with the privileges of Israel. Judaism would have denied itself had it yielded these things. When the apostles heard, therefore, the saying of Jesus that he had come to give his life in ransom, they heard already the death-knell of the ancient sacrifices—though it might require the complete destruction of the Holy Place to make them realize it.[2]

So far we have tried to show that although the Law held the normally appointed means of expiation, there was a pneumbra as it were of private suffering that could share the same purpose. But we ask now if it be not possible that the Law itself could be moving towards the vicarious expiation by one person; or rather we ask if, in view of the subsequent facts, we can find a place for the Law in God's completed scheme—for the Law not abrogated but fulfilled. For an answer to this question we go to St Paul.[3]

In Jewish eyes Paul was an apostate from Israel; Paul was sure he was not. On the contrary, he held that he was offering to his countrymen what he had received from God: a perception of Israel's true dignity and destiny, a penetration of God's word in Law and Prophets which ensured the Law's permanent value and made it sublime.

---

[2] Cf. M. J. Lagrange, *Le Messianisme*, pp. 236-251.

[3] Principally in chapters 5-8 of the Epistle to the Romans.

And yet Paul had to work out his new position in anguish of mind and heart. It is difficult for a Christian to measure the intensity of the shock this zealous Jew received on the Damascus road. In a flash of vision he discovered that one who had been crucified and thus under the Law's curse ('Cursed is every one that hangs on a tree' he had learned from Deuteronomy 21:23 cf. Gal 3:13), that same one had become alive and glorified. He now saw even further than his own prudent master Gamaliel who had said in the Sanhedrin: 'Let them alone; for if the work be of men it will come to naught, but if it be of God you cannot overthrow it'. He saw further, because that vision had made neutrality impossible. Henceforth he was committed: mistakenly the Jew would say but surely, he must admit, honestly. Remember that Saul was a Jew, zealous for the Law; remember that others, also zealous for the Law, had a hand in the death of Christ and were even now pursuing Christ's followers. Remember on the other hand how the vision had shown that the death was accepted and acceptable and the persecution condemned: 'Why do you persecute me?' A living and glorious Jesus made himself one with his dying and disgraced followers. 'What', thought Saul, 'must have become of the Law's curse when the curse has become such a living blessing?' In that hour the problem was born that Paul was to wrestle with in the next twenty years. Hitherto he had looked to the Law for life, searching the Scriptures in which he believed to find life; henceforth he is to look for life from the one who was put to death. What then was the Law? That it was God-given he must always believe; that it was the ultimate goal of the search he could no longer believe. The dilemma seemed to be placed before him: the Law or the Cross. We shall see how he decided there was no dilemma at all, and made an article of his creed: the Law *and* the Cross.

The tension in St Paul's mind reveals itself in sentences apparently contradictory. 'What is the Law?' He answers once: 'The Law is holy and just and good'. At another time his answer is: 'The Law is the min-

istration of death, of condemnation'. How can these
two statements be reconciled? Doubtless it is true to
say that Paul came to realize how even though a law
may be given by God it still remains a law and can
only condemn, not reward. ('Penalty for improper
use: £5' we find in our railway carriages; never 'Reward for proper use: £5'). But this view does not
satisfy or exhaust Paul's mind, because he goes further
and states that the Law, holy though it is, plays a positive part in the activity of sin: 'The Law entered in to
multiply sin', 'What gives power to sin is the Law'.
Such expressions may possibly be justified by crediting
Paul with the thought that the Law, adding so many
prescriptions to the law of nature, multiplied the possibilities of infringement. They may be even more
convincingly explained by the thought which Paul
himself puts forward, namely that a law turns what
would otherwise be good faith into bad faith: 'Where
there is no law there is no transgression', he writes.
Yet we leave all these explanations with a feeling of
dissatisfaction, because though they account for those
passages in which Paul speaks of the Law as an occasion of sin, they do not meet the needs of the texts
which make of the Law not an occasion but a cause,
and not of sin but of death.

To appreciate Paul's theological argument here we
could do worse than take a hint from his own dramatic
presentation in chapters 5, 7 and 8 in his Epistle to
the Romans. But first, by way of introduction to the
play, it might be wise to say something about the word
'redemption', for the idea is involved here, however
obliquely. 'A buying back', but from what or from
whom? It is unthinkable theologically that God should
owe, however vicariously, to the devil. To whom can
God owe anything but to himself? And here we already see how our language begins to stumble and
how we shall have to talk in metaphors, as St Paul
is forced to do. There is a divine reality which is God's
reconciling of man through the death of his son, but
the word and idea of 'redemption' remain a human
metaphor and a human concept. The image is strik-

ing and exact but not exhaustive; it is dramatic and must not be pushed to logical conclusions. It is important to notice also that the Pauline presentation we are about to describe is objective and juridical, a world view of the great religious phases of human history, and must not be taken for a peep into the single human soul. At its end we shall find that God 'buys us back' from the demand of his own justice ('sin merits death') as it is laid down in the Mosaic Law which God himself sponsored. We shall find also that some light, from one particular angle, will be shed on the truth that the old order is 'fulfilled' in the new.

The Characters. *Hamartia,* or Sin, King Thanatos' mistress. She is ugly but seductive and, oddly enough, least dangerous when veiled. The veil hides her true character of rebel against God. *Thanatos,* or Death, is crowned King of Body until the world's end, in the first scene of Act I. He would be king of Soul also, but to accomplish this Hamartia unveiled, known for what she is, must seduce Man. *Ego,* or Man—St Paul's 'Ego' is not himself nor any given individual: he is Humanity as it lives through the successive phases of religious history: humanity unfallen; fallen despite the clear command of Eden; fallen but ignorant as yet of the Law; fallen though knowing the Law; redeemed. *Nomos,* or Mosaic Law, is a severe and conscientious judge; he inflexibly declares the vindicatory sentence of God's 'justice'. Lastly *Christos,* our Lord himself, the living and dying expression of the fuller sense of God's 'justice', that is to say of 'justice-mercy' which demands death but not without ensuing life.

The Prologue. The scene is the upper and filthy air to which Hamartia and Thanatos enter dancing. They embrace.

Hamartia: Thanatos, where is thy sting?
Thanatos (holding her admiringly at arm's length):
The sting of Thanatos is Hamartia.
Hamartia: Yet Hamartia reigns by grace of Thanatos, and Thanatos is Hamartia's reward.

Thanatos: But Hamartia shall bring forth fruit to Thanatos. Without her he is nothing. Should she die, Thanatos dies too.

(Exeunt, rapturously)

Act I. Scene 1. Eden. Ego discovered. Hamartia lurking veiled.

Thanatos in the wings.

Voice: You shall not eat! (These words tear the veil from Hamartia. She advances to Ego who embraces her).

Voice: In the day you eat, you die. (Hamartia beckons to Thanatos who lays hold of Ego).

Voice: By one man Hamartia entered into the world and, by Hamartia, Thanatos.

Scene 2. The fallen world before the Law. Thanatos discovered throned; Hamartia at his side, veiled once more. Ego in the foreground.

Thanatos: And so Thanatos reigns from Adam to Moses and beyond, King of Body—and of Soul too, if Hamartia prevail unveiled.

Hamartia: But Hamartia may not yet appear Hamartia.

Ego: I do not know Hamartia.

Hamartia: Receive me then, unknowing. (Ego embraces her.)

Thanatos: And so is he my subject.

Voice: But not your slave. Ego has not sinned, knowing, after the likeness of Adam. Thanatos may touch him but not sting, not utterly destroy.

Ego: I live at least in part for, without command, I do not know Hamartia for what she is.

Act II. The scene is Israel. Enter Nomos to Hamartia (still veiled) and to Thanatos crowned and meditating further malice. Ego, somewhat dazed, in the foreground.

Nomos (in a loud voice): That Hamartia might appear Hamartia! (He tears away her veil, revealing her ugliness).

Ego (not appalled but hesitant): I did not know Hamartia but for Nomos.

Hamartia (not doubting the issue): By favour of Nomos I am now myself. Choose me for what I am. Choose me as Adam chose. (Ego chooses her)

Lament: Without Nomos Hamartia was dead, Ego alive.

With Nomos Hamartia came alive, Ego died.

Thanatos: For the wages of Hamartia is Thanatos.

Ego: Hamartia taking occasion from Nomos has killed me.

Nomos: The letter kills. I am the reluctant minister of Thanatos.

(Nomos retires upstage)

Ego (ruled now by Hamartia possessing his 'flesh' but still admonished by the higher, 'inward' man): In my flesh dwells not that which is good, yet I delight in the law of God according to the inward man. The good which I will I do not; the evil which I will not, that I do. Unhappy man that I am! Who will deliver me from this flesh foredoomed to Thanatos?

Voice: The grace of God through Jesus Christ!

Act III. The scene is Jerusalem on a Friday afternoon. Enter Nomos robed as a judge, prepared to hand over Ego to Thanatos.

Nomos: By the works of Nomos Ego cannot be made just. Nomos is powerless against Hamartia but can and must condemn the flesh she inhabits. I pronounce sentence of death on those under Nomos, under the Law.

Christos (coming forward): Made of a woman, made under the Law.

Nomos: My authority is over all.

Christos: You would have no authority were it not given from above. Your justice is God's; God interprets it.

Choir: Christ Jesus whom God has presented as a propitiation for the showing of his justice.

Voice: My justice is mercy; my chastisement expiation; my death life.

Nomos (stubborn): I am a minister of condemnation, no more.

Voice: Condemn then.

Christos: It is finished!

Nomos: Then am I satisfied. (There is darkness and a shout of triumph from Thanatos; but Ego looks up in hope and struggles in his grip).

Choir: That which Nomos was powerless to do
        God has done.
        Having sent his own son
        in the likeness of the flesh of sin
        he has condemned sin in the flesh,
        that the verdict of Nomos might be fulfilled.

Christos (rising from death): By one man came Thanatos: by one man freedom from Thanatos.

Voice: There is now therefore no condemnation for them that are in Christ Jesus.

Thanatos: My bond! I will have my bond! It has been written: 'The wages of Hamartia is Thanatos'.

Voice: All has been paid. Listen!

Ego's Song: Granting the demand of Nomos,
        God has cancelled the certificate of debt
        drawn up against us.
        He has annulled it, nailing it to the cross.

Christos: I am the certificate of debt, receipted. I am the payment, satisfied. I am the curse incurred and exhausted.

Thanatos (king still of body but not of soul): And yet I rule. Men die.

Choir: God has put all the enemies of Christos under
        his feet.
        And the enemy Thanatos shall be destroyed at
        the last.

Ego (smiling as he dies): Thanatos! Where is thy sting?

Choir: Buried with him by baptism
        in the likeness of his death,
        so shall we be
        in the likeness of his resurrection.

With Christ nailed to the Cross
the verdict of Nomos is fulfilled in us also.
Yes, we establish the Law,
and thus God is at once just and justifying.
Thanks be to God
who has given us the victory
through our Lord Jesus Christ.

To sum up prosaically: man could not plead ignorance for the first sin—Adam was confronted with an explicit divine command; knowing fully what sin was, he nevertheless accepted it and therefore incurred death: 'By one man Sin entered into this world and, by Sin, Death'. But this original command now, as it were, fades and the explicit command of the Law has not yet come; generations subsequent to Adam are considered ignorant, 'sin was not imputed when there was no Law'; if they were in death's power it was not through their own fault but through Adam's: 'yet death reigned from Adam to Moses even over those who had not sinned by a (conscious) transgression like Adam's'. But with the coming of the Law there is explicit command once again: the breaking of the Law is therefore a sin like Adam's and earns death in its own right, the Law itself is as it were the hanging judge ('the letter kills'). The Law can be satisfied only by death—though indeed it can demand death only of its own subjects. To satisfy this demand Jesus, 'made under the Law', steps forward 'Christ has bought us back from this condemnation of the Law, having become a condemnation for us (i.e., in our stead)'. The Law therefore remains good—it is the expression of God's will and the executor of his justice. As Paul sees it, the death of Christ explains the function of the Law.

But this was not the end. Recall that St Paul had seen this death turned to life; he had heard this Living One identify his followers with himself, living therefore with the same life. This for him resolved the enigma. He saw now into that divine plan which paradoxically combined justice with mercy: the two great

attributes of God are saved and God is revealed as
'both just and justifying'. The Law was good and
holy: in the name of God it denounced sin and pronounced its death-sentence. But being a law, it could
go no further: it could deal death but the subsequent
life must come from God. God had established a two-
edged system or retribution: once granted man's fail-
ure, God could not but intend the only alternative to
reward — condemnation. But he intended this condemnation to serve his merciful purpose. The condemnation would fall on the Crucified and secure its
due effect, the destruction of sin and therefore of sin's
accomplice, death. Death destroyed death.

These ideas are not a theological web artfully woven
by later Christian thinking: they are an integral part
of Paul's own solution for they satisfy his scattered
texts and one key text in particular which had long
been the subject of dispute. The interpretation of this
text (Rom 8:3-4) is that of Père Benoit in the article
we have quoted:

> That which the Law was powerless to do,
> a powerlessness it had by reason of the flesh,
> God having sent his own son
> in the likeness of the flesh
> and with the conquest of sin in view
> condemned sin in the flesh,
> in order that the death-sentence (*dikaioma*) of the
> Law might be fulfilled in us
> who do not walk according to the flesh
> but according to the spirit.

The Law, writes Paul, was powerless to condemn sin
in the flesh. It could indeed pronounce sentence of
death on man the transgressor, but that death would
not mean the defeat of sin: it would mean rather the
acknowledgement of sin's power. The death of the
body would leave untouched the supra-corporal oc-
cupying power which is sin. The Law had power only
over the body. Accordingly, Paul goes on, God sent
his son to die (for this is the meaning of 'sent'). The
Son though incarnate was not in the flesh of sin; he

was in the likeness of the flesh of sin. That is to say, the innocent body of Christ was juridically made capable of suffering in place of guilty flesh. What is the result? That the death-sentence passed by the Law meets its satisfaction (is 'fulfilled') in the Crucified, and this by God's deliberate will, not by any personal debt of the innocent Christ.

But is it fulfilled in him alone? Paul thinks not. 'That the death-sentence of the Law might be fulfilled *in us*', he writes, 'who do not walk according to the flesh but according to the spirit'. In other words, the verdict realized in Jesus is the same verdict as is realized in us Christians by reason of our union with him. One remembers the frequency on Paul's pen of the expression 'in Christ', and the apostle's doctrine of union with Christ by faith and baptism—the latter particularly uniting us with the death of Christ. With Christ all Christians are nailed to the Cross. The Law is satisfied not in one only but in a multitude united with him—we recall that the Vision had said, 'Why do you persecute *me*'. In the one and in the many the 'sin in the flesh' is destroyed. In principle the Christian is guided not by the flesh but by the spirit, not by the old dying and sin-infested thing but by the Principle of life himself.

St Paul therefore had found his own solution to the dilemma. He could and does say that now Christ has come the Law is in one sense 'that which is done away', 'that which is made void'. But when he declares that Christ is 'the end' of the Law he does not simply mean that the Law is abrogated, he means that the Law is satisfied—Christ is the goal of the Law. And so the Law remains, remains for all to see: it is 'the certificate of our debt' nailed for ever to the Cross. When we look at the Crucifix and say, 'the Law did this', do not let us forget that if the Law had a hand in Christ's death, as Paul's theological thinking views it, it had a hand also in our redemption; this, because in God's decree our life came precisely from his death. It is no contradiction to say that the Law is at once just and holy and at the same time is the minister of death. It is both of these things: precisely because it is the minister of death it is, in God's design, just and holy.

At the beginning of this chapter we accused Marcion of caricature. Perhaps a little unfairly; unfairly, that is, if he had in mind the Jewish conception of the Law. For even today it seems to the Christian that Judaism tends to think more of the divine justice than of the divine mercy. The Christian believes that this tendency is encouraged if the Old Testament is taken as God's last word, that the insistence on Law distracts from the tenderness of God which, as we shall see, is a theme of the Old Testament itself. And here we may be allowed to wander somewhat from our point. The Christian in his prayers does not plead for justice but always for mercy. He believes that his attitude to God is of a child to an indulgent father. Knowing God's kindness he can never be astonished at God's gifts—and the supreme gift is of God's own son. But it is a true gift. It is not that one comes to suffer where we should have suffered: it is more than that. The suffering is truly 'vicarious', that is to say, it expiates as our own suffering could never have expiated of itself. But in another sense it is not merely vicarious. With Christ all humanity is nailed to a cross. We are not absolved from the cross. But we hold that it is not our crucifixion, insofar as it is our crucifixion, that draws life from God; it is the crucifixion of the Son with whom in the eyes of God and by his inexplicable operation we are identified.

The Cross is the junction of the Old Testament and New: at that point they meet. By Christian faith in the Cross we do not destroy the Law, we establish the Law—that is to say, we set the Law on its feet, we lay it on lasting foundations. The new life that comes from faith in the Crucified gives to the Law, as the Christian sees it, its true value as an effective and fruitful remedy against sin. When Jesus is called the 'justice' (*dikaiosune*) of God, we have to understand that word in all the richness of its content: not legal justice only but saving mercy also.

Christ satisfies the legal justice because he sustains the Law's verdict; but he is also the manifestation and embodiment of God's constant and merciful will to save. We account man to be justified not now indeed through the works of the Law, but he is justified through the work of the Law as we have described that work. After the manner of the expiatory Old Testament sacrifices, the sacrifice of Christ has satisfied once for all the demands of extrinsic justice which God had committed to the Law; but at the same time it has brought the positive gift of life and intrinsic justness that the Law was incapable of providing.

Do we destroy the Law by faith? God forbid! We establish the Law.

The Cross is the great stumbling-block of Israel —as it is for less profound reasons of others; it is evidently here, if anywhere, that the Word of God has been found to falter, to be inconstant: it was Paul's temptation to believe it so. If Israel accepts the Cross she will come to understand it and if she understands it she will understand the Law. Marcion had not the excuse that Israel has. Nor have we.

CHAPTER 6

The Constant Word (2)

WE have seen something of Marcion's dilemma: how the Old Testament was too fierce for the New, how impossible it was to believe that the God of Jacob was the God of Jesus. He might have considered the sometimes alarming severity of the gospels themselves; or he might have studied, for example, the saving and forgiving aspect of God's Word which is a feature of the book of Deuteronomy. In either case the contrast would have been at least reduced. Instead, he chose to concentrate on his Old Testament 'God of Wrath'. Now it would be dishonest to deny the Old Testament presentation of Israel's warrior-God, establishing his people by conquest, admonishing them with chastisement. (We have spoken of this in our second chapter.) But we must beware of a one-sided picture. A father may love and punish, and punish because he loves. So it may be with the Word of God. At least let us check Marcion's judgment by the texts. To do this within a few pages we shall take one image that is, admittedly, most damaging to the heretic's thesis. One may be excused, because it is not only damaging but quite destructive. It has this further advantage, that it runs into and through the New Testament and reaches its climax there—indeed it runs right through into the Church's living, which is the continued expression of God's Word.

When the infinite Creator undertakes to make himself known to the finite creature, what happens? One might say that he cannot reveal himself fully: only the infinite can know the infinite, and it is unthinkable that the infinite should strive to achieve what is intrinsically contradictory. Yet in some mysterious way—and the act of revelation is in the

realm of the mysterious—communication is possible
between the divine and the human. That it does in
fact take place can only be because God wills it so;
that it *can* take place is equally God's doing: God
has so constituted the human finite creature, unlike
other finite creatures, that it is capable of some
glimpse of the infinite. 'Let us make man to our own
image and after our own likeness'; these words mean
nothing if they do not imply some general likeness
to God that the beasts have not, a likeness to God in
what we call the specifically human faculties: a
something which man has in common with God that
gives him dominion over the brutes, a something we
may presume which, from some bestowed capacity
of mind or heart or person, ranges man at the side
of God as other creatures are not, and so gives him
some sympathetic resonance to the divine.

Yet it remains that only the infinite can compre-
hend the infinite; and man, however Godlike, is finite.
But who is speaking of 'comprehension'? For lack
of a better term we have spoken of 'resonance', sympathetic vibration by which the human creature is, so
to speak, 'tuned' to God, receptive of God's wave-
length because God has made him so. There are
mental images of which the human being is capable,
images which (if communicated by God) can lead
man to some pictorial representation of the infinite
that is not entirely without value. Though God appears in a thick cloud, man's face glows with it. In
the graphic biblical phrase, man sees God from
behind.

But not, in this world, face to face. Man is only
the image of God, he and his companions; and so in
this image and in the relationships of this image he
discerns that of which these are the reflection. It is
this alone of which he is capable, and to this God's
self-revelation to man is restricted. But the revelation is not restricted to one facet of the image, nor
are all these of the same colour: indeed one picture
may, if held down to the human level, flatly contradict the other. Thus it is of the same God that these

two things are true: 'Man cannot see my face and live', and 'Blessed are the clean of heart, for they shall see God'. If we may change our metaphor, we may think of so many beams of light, each a different colour of the spectrum, all converging to one point: in this point they are reassembled to form one white light too bright for the eyes to sustain, but in the very blink this forces there is a glimpse not of itself but of a new colour, like the bright green we see when we close our eyes immediately after staring at the sun when it sets.

Let us take an example. We say that 'God is Love', not merely that without qualification or restriction he is 'loving'. What do we mean? The word 'love' here is an assemblage of all the related converging colours that God's self-revelation has afforded us. Of these the Father image is the most familiar to us in the Bible. In the book of Isaias we read:

You are our father.
Abraham does not acknowledge us.
Jacob no longer remembers us.
It is you, O God, who are our father.

And yet God is mother, too—the prophet even dares to refer to the breast of God where Israel is suckled, and he continues:

Like a son whom his mother cherishes,
so will I cherish you.

And most improbable of all, God is a child also in the fullness of time. All these kinds of love that we know in our own way, God in his own way exercises. All these familiar human pictures superimpose in our portrait of God; all these rays of varying colours suffuse each other and merge: God is not a loving father, a loving mother, a loving child: God is Love. However short our minds fall of this formulation, however difficult it may seem to reconcile omnipo-

tent love with the suffering of the beloved, this at
least we know of God: that he is the very opposite
of hate, that if human love is a poor affirmation of
what is divine, human hate is its very negation.

Now in God's very effort, if we may so speak, to
make us understand according to our mean capacity
what this love is—or rather, for the Scriptures are
very practical, what it means to us—he has recourse
to a figure that we would never have ventured upon.
Its riches are proved by the use the greatest mystics
have made of it, St John of the Cross for instance,
and the great Teresa. The image lies half way, so to
say, between the presentation of God as father and
the incarnation of God as child. I mean that it eases
the passage from the quite natural idea of God the
creator as father to the quite extraordinary idea of
God as child, as son of man. Because it was in effect
God's love for Israel his spouse that gave to the
world a child who was at once son of Israel and son
of God.

There is scarcely need to call attention to the bold-
ness of the husband-image when Genesis itself describes husband and wife as 'two in one flesh'. That
God and man should be so described is all but in-
tolerable—and yet the Old Testament implies it. We
shall see what this astounding idea is to lead to in the
New Testament after we have seen its origins and
development in the Old.

God's revelations are not a shout but a breath:
they do not deafen his prophet but breathe through
a heart and mind enriched as they are already with
the shape of their own experience and with the pattern of their own meditation. Revelation does not
destroy nature; it raises it. So it was with the prophet
Osee who preached in the northern kingdom seven
centuries before Christ. It was in the shape of his
great sorrow that the revelation came. He had married a wife whom he loved well and she left him.
But his love remained. He sought her still and at
last he found her and, having found, chastised her to
try her newly-promised fidelity; and in the end he

took her back. In all of this, the religious mind of the fierce and tender prophet saw a picture of Israel's treatment of her God. It is from human coldness that the prophet's mind is taken to the warmth of God's forgiving love; it is from the ugly word 'adultery' that the loveliest image in the whole of the Scriptures is born.

Israel's infidelity, her adultery, is to flirt with false gods, with Astarte and Baal. There had indeed been a short time of honeymoon with God, the forty years in the desert, though even that had not been without its quarrels. But this was over:

> She is no longer my wife,
> and I no longer her husband.
> Let her wipe the prostitute's marks from her face,
> take the adulterous amulets from her breast,
> or I will strip her naked
> as on the day she was born.

But God waits patiently and humbly till she tires of her lovers, or rather (and here is the very depth of God's humility) until they tire of her:

> She shall chase after her lovers and not catch up
>   with them,
> she shall seek and not find them.
> Then she will say:
> 'I will go back to my first husband,
> for I was happier then than now.'

The thought reminds us of that other picture of God's astounding humbleness when he runs out to meet the Prodigal who was still so selfish:

> Here I am dying of hunger;
> I will arise therefore ('therefore'!)
> and go to my father.

And so God welcomes the erring wife back and takes her on a second honeymoon:

Therefore I will attract her
and take her into the desert
and speak to her heart.

'Then', says the prophet in God's name:

She shall call me 'Husband'. . . .
I will wed her to me for ever
in tenderness and love. . . .
Her who was once called Unloved I will love
and she shall call me 'My God'.

One hundred years later, the prophet Jeremias takes up the same theme, this time indignantly:

If a man dismiss his wife
and she leave him and marry another,
has she the right to return to him?
And do you who have taken many a lover
think you can return to me?

But after the reform that followed this same prophet's denunciation, Jeremias joyously proclaims:

Come back, virgin Israel, come back to your
home.
How long will you be restless, undutiful child?
For God has worked a new wonder on earth:
The Wife has come back to her Husband.

But it is left to Ezechiel, some forty years after Jeremias, to develop the allegory at greatest length, to Ezechiel whose tongue was the most robust of all the prophets. Israel was an unwanted infant when God passed by and saw her; and he took her up and washed and cared for her. And she grew up and God clothed and adorned her. But she fell in love with her own beauty and played the harlot, flirting with Egypt, with Assyria, with Babylon, and all their gods. It is the eve of Jerusalem's destruction, and in Ezechiel's allegory there is no word of Israel's return to her Spouse after all this ingratitude:

Now then, you prostitute,
hear the word of the Lord.
Because you have flaunted your shame,
I will gather together all your lovers.
They shall take your garments and your jewels
and leave you naked.

But underneath this invective it is not difficult to
hear the note of disappointed love: God condescends
to be jealous; or rather, to return to what we said
at the beginning, the image of jealous love is called
to assist our understanding of what God's love for
man really means. At least we see how wide of the
mark it is to speak of the Old Testament God as
the God of Wrath.

We cannot end our survey of the Old Testament
on this unhappy note; nor is it necessary, because
the last word on this broken marriage is said on the
eve of Israel's return home after the Babylonian
exile. It is a word of forgiveness. We read in that
part of *Isaias* we call the Book of the Consolation
of Israel:

Fear not.
You shall forget the shame of your youth,
for your husband is your creator,
and his name is the Lord of Hosts.
Yes, as an abandoned wife whose heart is broken,
the Lord calls you back to him.
Does a man reject the wife of his youth?
says the Lord your God.
I left you for a little while,
but now, greatly pitying, I take you back.

And so we approach the new era with the hope of
a new and beloved Jerusalem where the divine bridegroom is to take his bride again and never let her
leave him. Let us now see if this marriage-theme is
taken up in the New Testament, by whom it is taken
up, and what is made of it—whether it fades away
or gathers force, whether it is impoverished or en-

riched. We must surely guess that one who said he
had come not to destroy but to fulfill would not neg-
lect this climax of the expression of God's love for
man.

Our Lord said of the Baptist that he was the last
great figure of the old order: 'The Law and the
Prophets are until John; after that, the Kingdom of
God is preached.' It is very fitting, therefore, that
this last voice of the Old Testament should take up
the ancient image and point to its fulfillment: 'I am
not the Christ', said John when his own disciples
complained of the progress Jesus was making, 'I am
only his joyful envoy':

> It is the bridegroom who has the bride;
> the friend of the bridegroom (John himself)
> rejoices at the voice of the groom.

The comparison of Jesus to a bridegroom is already
unexpected enough; it is still more surprising that
the bride appears. Who is she? Here surely we must
conclude that the Baptist's words suppose the Old
Testament background and that the bride is Israel.
But if this is true, it is difficult to avoid the implication that Christ is supposed to have assumed the
rôle that God himself played in the Old Testament
wedding-image: the partner of God's wedding with
Israel is now seen to be the human nature of his
Word. What precisely this implication further involves we shall have to wait to see.

And our Lord himself appropriates the bridegroom
metaphor. It will be remembered that the Baptist's
disciples challenged Jesus and his disciples for refusing to observe the fast. Our Lord replied:

> Can the friends of the bridegroom mourn
> while the groom is with them?
> The days will come when the groom is snatched
>   away,
> and then they will fast.

This is the time of Christ's wooing of Israel, a time which he himself later describes in two of his parables as a wedding-feast.

The gospels therefore lay the foundation for the future building upon this metaphor. It is left to St Paul, and later to the Apocalypse, to develop the image and to take soundings of its profundity.

In the second epistle to the Corinthians, which we may place about 57 A.D., Paul compares himself not to the friend of the bridegroom, as John had done, but rather to the father of the bride. For he is addressing the church of Corinth, the child of his own foundation:

> I am jealous of you with God's own jealousy,
> for I have wedded you to one single husband,
> a pure virgin to be presented to Christ.

It should be recalled that for Paul the Christians are the true heirs of Abraham, the new Israel, the 'Israel of God'. It will be noticed how the image has become more explicit, and how the wedding of the old Israel to God is assumed to have its true fulfilment in the wedding of the new Israel to Christ. It will be observed also how being pleasing to Christ, being an acceptable bride, has become a motive of the spiritual life. This is no wrench of God's own prerogative because, as St Paul says, 'God was in Christ reconciling the world to himself'.

But it is in the epistle to the Ephesians that St Paul opens his mind most generously, and his words are reminiscent of Ezechiel's great allegory of God and Israel. As usual, Paul is not developing a dogma for its own sake but rather pointing a moral lesson, here the lesson of ideal relations between Christian husband and wife. There is a parallel, he says, between human marriage and the union of Christ with his Church; the two states help to explain one another. Christ can be said to be the spouse of the Church because she is his by right of conquest, and he cherishes her as his own body. He goes on:

Husbands, love your wives as Christ loved the
Church: he delivered himself up for her in order
to make her holy by cleansing her in the bath of
water with an accompanying word. For he wished
her to appear before him all resplendent, without
spot or blemish but holy and unstained.

This passage echoes Ezechiel because there, too,
God found Israel and bathed her in water to prepare
her as his bride—the custom in the ancient East. In
this present passage there is no doubt that the bath-
ing with the 'accompanying word' is an allegory of
Baptism with its formula. By this effective ceremony
conferred 'in the name of Jesus', Christ takes possession of the baptized who is thus taken into the Israel
of God.

But St Paul goes further and pushes the metaphor
to its astonishing extreme, invoking in support the
ancient definition of marriage:

Husbands must love their wives
just as they love their own bodies.
Now no one hates his own flesh,
no, he feeds it and takes good care of it.
This is exactly what Christ does for the
    Church. . . .
'A man therefore must leave his father and mother,
to cling to his wife;
and the two are but one flesh'.
This mysterious text is of great moment
because it applies to Christ and the Church.

The climax of the comparison, 'two in one flesh',
should not be allowed to escape attention. No doubt
it is already latent in the Old Testament allegory, but
to state it is to shock—deliberately. Indeed, in the
Old Testament such a thing could hardly be said and
be rightly understood. In the New it is different,
because by now it is known that the Word has been
made flesh; in this one flesh God and man are
united. We may take the matter even further, though

here even the marriage symbol is outstripped, by
calling upon the fourth gospel:

> He who eats my flesh
> and drinks my blood
> remains in me
> and I in him.

This is how Christ feeds the Church. This is how
they become two in one flesh.

The glory of the solemn wedding is however still
to come. The book of Isaias had looked forward to
Israel's wedding with God. It makes her say:

> I rejoice in the Lord,
> my soul is joyful in my God;
> because he has clothed me with salvation,
> covered me with a robe of justice,
> like a bride who adorns herself with jewels.

The Apocalypse no less looks forward to the great
and final triumph. And the bridegroom? The Lamb:

> Now is the wedding-feast of the Lamb;
> his bride has adorned her beauty,
> she has been clothed in a robe of shining white.

And to the question: 'Who is the bride?' he answers
as the prophet before him had answered: 'Jerusalem'.
But it is a heavenly and purified Jerusalem who is
the bride of the Lamb, Christ:

> I saw a new heaven and a new earth. . . .
> And I saw the Holy City, the new Jerusalem,
> coming down from heaven, from God:
> she has adorned her beauty
> like a young bride ready for her husband.
> And I heard a voice from the throne cry:
> Behold the dwelling of God with men!

And still the last word is not said. The bold reve-

lation has been made, but like all that God shows of
himself it has not yet been nor ever will be mastered.
When it is accepted, that is to say lived, it grows
without ceasing in the one who receives: appetite
grows by what it feeds on. We have to await heaven
to find the fullness of the reality hidden behind the
image. Yet some taste of this we already find in the
writings of those who knew best because they have
lived with this gift of God and nourished their lives
on the thought of it. One might be tempted to say
that the great discovery of the mystics was that this
image of marriage could be applied not only to the
Church as a whole but to each individual member
in particular. The step had been taken towards this
by St Paul himself. Provoked by the vices of certain
Corinthians he writes:

> Do you not know that he who unites himself with
> a harlot makes one body with her? For it is said:
> The two shall be one flesh. But he who unites
> himself to the Lord is one spirit with him.

Here again the comparison is shocking but instructive. The mystics turn it to their own account. In
doing so they have a sure instinct, for in the whole
range of biblical images there is not one that so
audaciously and so significantly paints for us the love
of God. Moreover, these saints realized that in
choosing God for their love they had lost no form of
human love, and certainly not the greatest love which
is at the heart of marriage.

Here is an example taken from perhaps the greatest of them all, at least in warmth of expression,
from St John of the Cross as he ruminates on the
Canticle of Canticles:

> Deep-cellared is the cavern
> of my love's heart. I drank of him alive.
> Now stumbling from the tavern
> no thoughts of mine survive,
> and I have lost the flock I used to drive.

He gave his breast; seraphic
in savour was the science that he taught;
and there I made my traffic
of all, withholding naught,
and promised to become the bride he sought.

My spirit I prepare
to serve him with her riches and her beauty;
no flocks are now my care,
no other toil I share;
and only now in loving is my duty.

So now if from this day
I am not found among the haunts of men,
say that I went astray
love-stricken from my way,
that I was lost but have been found again.[1]

To such a conclusion the word that was spoken
through Osee could come, but it is a word that he
and Ezechiel and Paul and John would understand.

[1] Translated by Roy Campbell.

CHAPTER 7

The Word in the Gospels

ALTHOUGH the historical approach to the Scriptures characteristic of the last two centuries has done some excellent work and left us with certain considerable advantages, it has nevertheless left behind it an unfortunate emphasis, a distraction from the theological message of the Scriptures. This fact is usually discussed against an Old Testament background, but it is clear that the discussion is relevant for the New Testament also because here, too, we are dealing with the Word of God—that is to say with a message of salvation. It is needless to say, of course, that the transference of the principle has to be made with the greatest care. There is, for instance, all the difference in the world between the committal to writing of a seven-hundred-year-old tradition about Abraham and a written account, perhaps as early as fifteen years after the event, of the main outlines of our Lord's career. And yet, once this has been said, it does remain true that the purpose of the evangelists themselves is less biographical than theological. It is enough to remember, or at least it is a symptom of this, that not one of the evangelists offers us a description of the Crucifixion itself but all four remark briefly: They crucified him. No doubt we are right in this connection to investigate all there is to be known of the Roman process of crucifixion for our own information and devotion and for the benefit of those we are called to teach, but even while we are doing so it would be well to bear in mind that we are doing what the evangelists did not do, and that the further we go along this line the more risk we take of missing the evangelists' primary lesson. And since we have mentioned this point rather at random it might be well to suggest

immediately, lest our approach seem negative, that
side by side with this historical research there must
go a theological and biblical reseaerch into the function of suffering in Old Testament and New. This
might sound idealistic and beyond the powers of a
busy teacher. It is not in fact. I am simply suggesting that when we come to the Crucifixion in the Passion story we should read for ourselves and for the
children the Song of the Suffering Servant in the
53rd chapter of Isaias, Psalm 21—begun by our Lord
himself on the Cross and so revealing to us his mind
—and the famous hymn to the Cross in the second
chapter of Philippians. Or, to take another example,
that we should spend at least as much time pointing
out that when our Lord walked the waters or calmed
the storm he was displaying the powers the Psalmist
ascribes to God, as to verifying the size and depth of
Lake Galilee. After all, the evangelist's conclusion
of the Storm episode is not 'How did he do it' but
'Who is this?' I believe that the approach just outlined is dictated to us by the literary form which we
call 'gospel'. It is therefore necessary to examine
what the word 'gospel' itself implies. Later we shall
discuss how the evangelists interpreted their task.

The first and most certain thing we all know about
the gospels is that there are four of them; and in a
sense this is the very thing we should try to forget;
to stress it leads to unfortunate consequences we
shall try afterwards to show. It is only fair to say
that the word 'gospels' in the plural dates back at
least to Justin in the second century. This makes it
respectable but not necessarily helpful. It is much
more useful to remember that there are not four
gospels but one gospel in four forms: the gospel according to Matthew, according to Mark, and so on.
The term gospel (early English god spel, good news)
closely translates the Greek *eu-aggelion* which in the
first half of the story is the good news brought by
Jesus Christ and then becomes the good news about
Jesus Christ. We have to do, therefore, not simply
with a record but with a message. Of this message

there are four presentations, four written forms, four written approaches to the one unwritten message.

This message is a religious one. Already in classical Greek the word *eu-aggelion* has a religious flavour: it meant the sacrifice offered on the receipt of good news, thanking the gods for the message which, usually, was proclaimed from the temple steps. In the first century before our Lord it came to mean the good news itself: but it is still religious in tone because it is commonly used of events connected with the 'divine' emperor—accession or victory or birth of a royal son, or a visit for which all roads to the privileged town were to be repaired, the paths made straight and the rough places plain. And it is not without interest that the bearer of such good news was greeted with the waving of palm-branches. But since the true literary background of our gospels is first and foremost the Old Testament, it is important to notice that there the subject of the 'good news' is the enthronement of God as king, that is to say the assertion by God of his royal rights and his coming as Saviour and Giver of Life. The prophet Isaias speaks of an 'evangelist' who tells the towns of Judah: Here comes your God, and proclaims how beautiful are the feet that bring good news, 'who announce salvation, who say to Sion: Your God is King'. Within the word itself, therefore, we have both a royal and a religious significance. But if the pagan emperors, to judge by so many of their coins, were styled 'Lord and Giver of Life', we have in the Christian use of the term 'gospel' an element of defiance—it is God who reigns, it is the gospel of the kingdom of God, it is God who is Lord, God who gives life. When St Mark, therefore, heads his work 'The beginning of the gospel of Jesus Christ', he is telling us that his book contains the news that God has determined here and now to display his kingship (this is the good news from Jesus Christ), and this through his son the appointed king, as Jesus himself claims before Pilate (this is the good news about Jesus Christ). And what this good news means to man is expressed clearly by our Lord himself when he deliberately chooses to read this passage from the prophet Isaias in the synagogue:

> The spirit of the Lord is upon me;
> he has sent me to bring the good news to the poor;
> to announce deliverance to the captive,
> new sight to the blind,
> freedom to the oppressed—
> a time of pardon from the Lord. (Luke 4:18-19)

It is the content of this good news, therefore, which must be our first concern, and I hope I am not being too mysterious if I sum it up by saying that it is better to teach the gospel than to teach the gospels. To speak practically and clearly, it is more important to spend our time on the common doctrine of the gospels than to spend it on explaining away their divergencies. We shall return to this question later, however.

The remarks we have just made will, I hope, serve to guide our general outlook, but, after all, we are faced also with more particular problems of gospel interpretation which, I think, cannot be adequately met without some knowledge of how our written gospels came into being. The vague idea that they are desk-compositions written at a sitting can do much harm in the field of interpretation. Against this unrealistic notion can always be quoted the prologue of Luke: Several people have undertaken to compose an account of the events that have taken place in our midst. . . . so I too have decided to write an ordered account. But even earlier than these apparently fragmentary attempts at written records came the apostolic preaching, the *kerygma:* in the beginning was the spoken word. The outline of this kerygma can be drawn from a comparison of the earliest apostolic speeches in the Acts of the Apostles with the Epistles of St Paul. Briefly, the earliest form this good news took is as follows: A descendant of David has recently moved about in Palestine doing good and showing by many 'works of power, prodigies and signs' that God was at work in him. He was put to death at the instigation of many of his own people but he rose again and sits enthroned at the right hand of God. From here he pours out the Spirit on his faithful ones and from here he will return to 'restore all things'. Here in a nutshell is the kerygma, the gospel. We notice immediately that what might be called the biographical element is reduced to a minimum and that the theological note is struck straight away. For the first sermons in the Acts are careful to point out that this is not just the career of a great Rabbi or even of the greatest of prophets; they insist that it is a unique career of which all the prophets spoke, towards which the whole of the Old Testament looked; the horrifying fact of the Crucifixion itself, they are anxious to note, was according to the 'determinate counsel and foreknowledge of God'; and as for the biographical events, they are but the necessary prelude to the present theological reality of the victorious and presiding Christ. It is important also to notice that this kerygma always closes with an appeal to repentance. I say it is important because it shows us that the purpose of proclaiming the good news was always practical, that the purpose of the gospels themselves, therefore, was not to convey idle information but to create an impact, to move the reader to repentance. This observation brings us back once more to the relative unimportance of biographical detail as compared with lasting spiritual results.

We may come now nearer to the gospels themselves which are an expansion of the kerygma. This is most noticeable in Mark. He does not speak of his own work as 'memoirs'—a term used of the gospels by some early writers—but as a 'gospel', that is to say (for the terms are interchangeable) as a kerygma. Like Peter in his first sermons Mark asserts in his first words that the career he is going to describe is a fulfilment of prophecy, like him he appeals for repentance: The time is fulfilled. . . . Repent and believe the good news. He then proceeds to describe in more detail how this Jesus 'went about doing good' and narrates how Jesus died and rose again. In Matthew and Luke the pattern is not so clear, though it is evidently there and Matthew even expands two elements of the kerygma not emphasized by Mark—namely, the fact that Jesus was a descendant of David and that he was the fulfilment of the prophets; but Matthew also departs from the primitive kerygma, by collecting so many of our Lord's sayings on moral matters—what the scholars call not kerygma but *didache,* not proclamation but doctrine. The question we ask ourselves now is how this development took place.

There is no doubt that the early Church could not long be satisfied with the bare outlines of the kerygma as we have described it, especially as those who had lived with our Lord had many things to recall that he had said and done. His sayings in particular would be carefully stored in their retentive memories: the disciples of every Jewish Rabbi were capable of that —and how much more of this much greater than a Rabbi? Thus the first three great discourses of Matthew would soon be formed — no doubt before the gospel itself came into being—I mean the Sermon on the Mount, the programme for Christian living, the Missionary Discourse, the programme for Christian preaching, and the Parable discourse, the presentation of the mystery of the Kingdom. This process would begin, doubtless, when the death of Stephen in A.D. 32 or 34 led to the dispersal of Christian missionaries; and in all of it memory played a large part. And since before printed books came to kill memory men picked up more with their ears than with their eyes, certain oral aids were used to assist memory—rhyme, rhythm, alliteration, striking formulae, repetition, graphic comparison. Our Lord, the wise teacher, pursued this method and distinct traces of it have come down to us in our present gospels—so many witnesses to the antiquity of their sources. Take repetition, for example. It is no impiety for us to confess that this makes wearisome reading for us, so long as we remember that it was not done to please us but to help the dis-

ciples. Take for instance our Lord's comparison of
the wise and the foolish man which could have been
put into half a dozen words; notice the balanced contrast and the measured, leisurely style, facilitating
memory:

He who hears my words and keeps them
is like a wise man
who built his house on a rock.
The rain fell,
the storm came,
the winds blew
and were let loose against that house.
And it did not fall,
because it was founded on a rock.

But he who hears my words and does not keep them
is like a foolish man
who built his house on sand.
The rain fell,
the storm came,
the winds blew
and beat upon that house.
And it fell,
and great was its fall. (Mt. 7:24-7)

Here surely we are in touch with the words as they
came from our Lord; this is not the manner of an editor but of a careful teacher. And he was indeed careful. By those who have examined our Lord's sayings
in the light of their original language (so far as this
is at present known) we are assured that they bear
the impress of well-prepared deliverances. In the
kindly sayings the sounds are soft and gentle: thus,
'Come to me all you who are heavy laden' is *etho
lewathi kullekon delahain ute'inin;* whereas, for example, when hypocrites are contrasted with simple
Christian disciples the sounds are strongly guttural
and mockingly sibilant: thus, 'As the hypocrites do
in the synagogues and streets' is *hekma da'abadu
shaqqarin bkenishatha ubeshuqin.* It is touching to
think, as we rarely think, that our Lord must have
worked hard to prepare all he had to say, for when

the Son of God became man he became like to us in
all things, sin alone excepted.

To return to the phenomenon we have noticed, that
of balance or parallelism: it is the characteristic of all
solemn Semitic speech and it pervades our Lord's discourses as reported in the gospels, thus showing the
fundamentally Jewish character of the sayings and
witnessing to the fidelity of the evangelists. This literary trick is sometimes helpful in interpretation or textual criticism of the Psalms, for example, and so it is
at times in the gospels. There is a well-known cou-
plet: Give not that which is holy to dogs. Throw not
your pearls before swine. Dogs and swine are plainly
parallel, but what of 'holy' and 'pearls'? The rule of
parallelism suggests a closer correspondence. And
here the original language comes to our aid. In Aramaic the word *qedasha* means 'holy' but the same
consonants vocalized *qudsha* means a golden ring. It
should be observed here that if we are reluctant to
admit a mistranslation on the part of an evangelist we
must at least recognize that the possibility brings us
very close to the Aramaic spoken word of our Lord
himself. In any case, it seems that Gospel interpretation in detail will receive in the future considerable
assistance from any further knowledge which may be
forthcoming of the actual language our Lord spoke.
Perhaps one of the most probable conjectures in this
field concerns the very odd sentence of Luke: Give
alms of what is inside, and then the outside will be
clean. Matthew's form of what is evidently the same
saying is: Clean the inside first and then everything
will be clean. But where did Luke's strange text come
from? Probably from a confusion of the two very
similar Aramaic words: *dakkau* to cleanse, and *zak-
kau* to give alms.

There is therefore powerful evidence that very
many of our Lord's words have been closely remembered and recorded, and there are certain units (like
the above example of the wise and the foolish man)
which have certainly been preserved as units. But is
this always so? It seems not. Thus for the Sermon on

the Mount in Matthew 5-7: does this represent one long and difficult discourse addressed to the patient crowds, or is it a collection and ordering of many separate sayings made by the evangelist or by someone before his time? If we are to judge by the way these same sayings are scattered throughout the gospel of Luke (and any Bible with a good reference system will show this) we should be at least prepared to admit the possibility of a collection made by someone anxious to systematize. If we remember further that Matthew's is the gospel of five great discourses, five books of the New Law as it were, we shall be inclined to say that the unity is artificial, the historical element has been sacrificed to the theological purpose—which, I remind you, is well in keeping with the nature of 'gospel'. This example has been chosen only because it illustrates a useful principle of gospel interpretation. We have often been warned, and wisely, that the context of a saying must always be taken into account. But we must always remember that the context first has to be proved, and the first misgiving we have is when we find a saying of one gospel in a different context in the next. Indeed, within this very Sermon on the Mount we have a notable example. I have read in certain books now, it is true, somewhat out of date, that our Lord must have taught his disciples the 'Our Father' on two separate occasions, for Matthew gives it at the beginning of our Lord's public life in the Sermon, and Luke at the end. This is frankly incredible since Luke introduces his own 'Our Father' with a request from the disciples: 'Lord teach us to pray'—are we to say they had forgotten? Perhaps the whole question of chronology is here irrelevant; it is certainly unimportant; but if not, I should unhesitatingly accept St Luke's placing for, apart from Matthew's general tendency to group, a glance at his chapter six with its strict arrangement of three sections with a repeated refrain: Alms in secret, Prayer in secret, Fasting in secret, interrupted by the 'Our Father' section, betrays an old arrangement now interfered with.

We have so far tried to look behind the gospels as it were. It is time now to look at the gospels as we have them now. For the last hundred years scholars have laboured to explain their strange similarities yoked to their no less surprising differences. The problem is not yet solved, indeed it has recently opened up all over again and what seemed an acquired solution (the dependence of Matthew and Luke on Mark) is again under fire. We can do no more here than state what seems to be the most likely solution and the one which is, at least in part, rallying more and more scholars to it. Briefly it is this: that behind the gospels in their present form stands an Aramaic tradition and, it appears, an Aramaic written gospel having much in common with our present Matthew, of which the apostle Matthew was the author. This primitive gospel may be as early as A.D. 45. Various translations were made of it into Greek and from separate members of this little family sprang our present gospels. This is putting the matter much too simply, of course, but it will serve our turn. This theory does not of course deny an interdependence between the three first gospels also.

It would not be worth our while to describe this process were it not that it has various consequences in the sphere of interpretation. It at least opens our eyes to a fact we asserted from the beginning and arrived at from a different point of view, namely that the gospel is one in many forms. This realization may have very practical results and so I dare here to propose what, except for one short experiment, I have not been able to put into practice myself. Namely, that we should teach the first three gospels not separately but all together. There are practical difficulties against this, of course, of which the greatest is the lack of a Catholic English text of all three gospels printed side by side—a 'Synopsis', as it is misleadingly called. The second is the lack of a commentary on all three gospels together, though Father Cox has made a most useful step in this direction for popular use at least. The advantages seem to me obvious: first, we do not

have to bore our students by treating the same incident or discourse three times in their course—instead
we see it once from all three angles, and therefore we
see it solid. Second, we secure a robust approach to
the vexed question of harmonization of which I shall
say a word in a moment. Third, we learn by contrast
of the different aims and characteristics of the various
gospels.

We have mentioned the thorny question of harmonization—more thorny for those who have not appreciated the literary form of which we are speaking
or for those who have taken no hint from the fact that
even the Beatitudes, the Pater, the inscription over
the Cross, the Eucharistic words themselves, are all
presented in different words in our different gospels.
We have already spoken of the fidelity in recording
our Lord's words, but there is also a certain freedom
used by each of the evangelists—as the texts themselves bear witness. I have read a learned article that
set out to prove that when Matthew and Luke make
our Lord forbid his missionaries a staff and Mark
makes him allow them a staff, the word 'staff' means
in one case an aid to walking, in the other a defensive
weapon—though in truth the Greek suggests no difference. But the truth seems to lie elsewhere: all three
are preaching complete detachment but Matthew,
with less sense of realism than Mark, makes this ex-
tend even to the poorest traveller's support. A similar
answer should be given, one feels, to the famous blind
man of Jericho problem: were there two or one, were
they or he cured as our Lord was on the way into or
on the way out of Jericho? Many would answer:
there were two, and therefore it can be said there was
one; and the miracle was worked on the way out of
the older Jericho but on the way into the new. As an
isolated solution this may not offend us, though it
sounds artificial, but when similar solutions are offered for similar difficulties one feels a sense of exegetical strain. Surely it is more natural to recall that
a 'gospel' is a theological literary form in which his-

torical detail may remain unemphasized and general statement admitted?

The same conclusion is arrived at, by a different route, in the school of interpretation known as Form Criticism which (to confine ourselves to our present purpose) has established one helpful conclusion amongst many other unacceptable ones, namely, that close analysis shows how the body of our first three gospels is composed of so many beads on a thread, of passages which can be displaced without losing their significance; the thread itself, that is to say the connecting passages whether concerned with place or with time, is of secondary value and is not meant to have any more. A comparison of the gospels between themselves bears this out. So, for instance, the healing of the leper in Mark appears out of the blue, as it were: Mark says simply, 'And a leper came'. Matthew however says, 'When he came down from the mountain a leper came'. Luke says, 'When he was in one of the cities a leper came'. One may multiply the lepers and the incidents, of course, though all three accounts suggest the same event; but it seems nearer the truth that the various indications are connecting links only—like the meaningless 'at that time' of the beginning of our Sunday gospels — links which are merely convenient methods of carrying on the narrative. If this is so, and the literary form of gospel is quite compatible with it, while the doctrine of Inspiration has nothing to say against it, we should be much more cautious of writing what are often called 'lives' of our Lord as if we possessed an ordered chronological account of his career instead of the good news of his redemptive work.

From what has been said I hope it does not appear that the interpretation of the gospels is destructive work, a work of demolition. The purpose is not to destroy but to fulfil. I repeat that the more we can know of the historical side of the Scriptures the better, but if such investigation means a loss to the theological side—as experience has taught us all that it does—then it must be allowed to fall into the background, because the gospels demand to be taken for what they are: not descriptions of life in Palestine over a period of two years, but the good and eternal news of God's salvation.

There is one last feature of modern interpretation that deserves mention because it may help us to intelligent understanding not only of the gospels but of the whole biblical literature. One of the most fashionable, and ugliest, words today is 'demythologization'. Now we must insist that though the word is new, the thing it represents is as old as man himself. When human beings think and speak of the Infinite God it is plain that all they have at their disposal is human language. They are perfectly aware, and the biblical authors themselves say so clearly, that the human tongue is inadequate to express what is divine. Consequently, even when they are using human descriptions of God, their mind is for ever deprecating the human expression and stripping it of its limitations; in other words they are taking what may be (unhappily) called 'mythical' elements out of it; they are 'demythologizing'. If I preach in England I may point up to heaven; if I preach in Australia I may do the same; but I presume this may be called the opposite direction. I feel no awkwardness about it, however, but what do I mean? That heaven is neither up nor down but all about us. I have demythologized on a small scale. But let me quote St Jerome from the fourth century to show that the thing is not new:

> In the Church, too, we have foolish speaking: as when a man, deceived by a passage in Isaias (6:4), a passage he has failed to understand, thinks that heaven is curved like an arch; that a throne, too, is placed in heaven and that God sat upon it, and that as though he were a judge or a general the angels stood in circle round about him to obey his instructions and to be sent on separate missions.

Here is demythologization with a vengeance—fifteen hundred years old.

CHAPTER 8

The Gospel of the Word

WHEN we speak of John the Theologian we mean that the fourth gospel, this *evangelium spirituale* as the Fathers called it, is more explicitly a theology than the first three. This does not mean that the fourth gospel is more difficult. On the contrary, I believe it is easier—because where the first three gospels only hint their theology, John states his. One might even dare to say that if we find the first three gospels easier, it is a sign that we have missed their theological message which is latent. It is wide of the mark to speak of the fourth gospel as supplementing the information of the first three; it is rather that it brings out for them explicitly a fourth, spiritual, dimension.

But let us begin at the beginning. The difference between John and his fellow evangelists leaps to the eye even if we consider not the formal approach but the material with which he works. Of all the miracles our Lord performed he mentions only seven, and only one of these is in common with the Synoptics, namely the multiplication of loaves. As for our Lord's shorter sayings, he has nothing, though they are so frequent in the other gospels. And although, as we shall see, his is a sacramental gospel, he describes neither our Lord's Baptism in the Jordan nor the institution of the Holy Eucharist. Nor does he touch on the usual moral questions of marriage, poverty and the rest. His main preoccupation is with fraternal charity: the verb or noun occurs forty-four times in John as against six in Mark—and we might observe in this connection that he speaks of God as Father one-hundred-and-eighteen times as against Mark's four. Statistics are lying things but statistics like these can scarcely be ignored. And as for the disputes about the Law which are a feature of the

other gospels, these hardly find a place in John. I say
'hardly' because a dispute on the Sabbath question
does arise in John, and it is instructive to contrast
our Lord's retort in John with that on a similar occasion in Mark. In Mark our Lord takes his stand
on precedent and, in true Rabbinic fashion, appeals
to the Biblical example of David; in John he rises to
another plane altogether, to a world far higher than
the Law, and his answer is 'My Father is working
every day of the week, so why shouldn't I?' This
example could stand as a parable of the difference
of approach.

There is another differentiating characteristic however which, though it has a common root with all the
others, is most enlightening of all. You will have
noticed how John never lets an incident go by without making our Lord explain its significance. If
Luke tells of the raising of a boy to life, our Lord
gives the boy to his mother and that is the end of it;
but when John tells of the raising of Lazarus, our
Lord follows with his discourse on the resurrection
and the life. When in Mark a blind man sees again,
that is the end of it too, except that the man follows
Jesus rejoicing; but when in John a blind man is
cured, our Lord takes occasion to announce himself
as light of the world. When all three Synoptics nar-
rate the multiplication of loaves, all eat, the frag-
ments are gathered up, and no more is said; but
when John tells of the same, we have the magnificent
following discourse on the Bread of Life. That is
what I mean by saying that the meaning is there in
the Synoptics but we are left to find it for ourselves.
With John we have no such complaint; he explains
what we should have concluded from the Synoptics
had we the insight, namely that if Jesus raises to life,
he must have an abundance of life in himself; that
if he restores the blind, he is himself the very source
of light, that if he creates the bread it comes entirely
from him, he is the bread of life.

Now John warns of this approach in the very first
line of his gospel. In the beginning was the *Word,*

and this Word was made flesh. Our Lord is so described nowhere but in the Johannine writings: in the gospel twice, in the first epistle and the Apocalypse once. We have already indicated the origin of this term and its Old Testament development. John means that the word of God which had sounded in the thunder and in the gentler creation, which had found a voice in the Law and on the lips of the Prophets, this same Word now at last took flesh. It follows that every movement of that flesh is itself a message from God, a word that tells man something about God; every one of its actions is a sign. It is not by accident that this last word 'sign' is John's word for miracle. Where the other gospels use the word *dunamis* or 'show of power', for the wonderful things our Lord does, John does not use it once; all those things are *semeia,* signs, that is to say meaningful actions. St Augustine puts it in his usual neat way: *Facta Verbi verba*—the actions of the Word are words. In this we have the key to the whole of John's gospel. This is what we mean when we say that his gospel is sacramental: it fills what is visible with significance and invisible efficacy. The flesh of the Word is the primal, visible thing; it is filled with the Word of God which communicates itself through that flesh—power goes out from it. (And here I would remind you again how the word of God is not just informative but creative.) That is why the famous Eucharistic chapter of John turns out to be the watershed of his gospel, the turning point, the testing ground, when all leave him but the Twelve. This must have been the central point of Christ's teaching —he would not have allowed all to go away for less. But we shall return to this discourse later. For the present I should like to illustrate John's method from his second, third and fourth chapters.

There are perhaps not two scholars who agree on the plan of the fourth gospel but we may take what seems to me a very probable hypothesis [1] and work

[1] That of C. H. Dodd in his *Interpretation of the Fourth Gospel* (Cambridge, 1953), a book of immense value.

with that. The body of the gospel—and by that I mean from the end of the introductory Chapter 1 to the beginning of the Passion narrative at the beginning of Chapter 13—seems to fall into seven episodes, each composed of one or two signs, that is to say meaningful incidents, and at least one discourse to explain the sign. The first episode [2] we choose for our illustration has two signs: the miracle of Cana and the Cleansing of the Temple; and there are two explanatory discourses: one with Nicodemus on the question of the new birth, the other with the Samaritan woman on the nature of the new worship in spirit and in truth. The common theme of these signs— and therefore of the discourses—is that of a change from old to new. John tells us that at Cana there were six water-pots; he adds significantly that they were 'for the purification of the Jews'. Now in John's vocabulary 'the Jews' always stands as an expression for the old order; it is almost equivalent to our word 'Jewry' and invites us to think less of individuals than of a régime. If in addition to this we remember that the Rabbis often used water for a symbol of the Law, we are prepared here for a symbolism over and above the historical event. Remembering further that our Lord in the Synoptic gospels refers to the new order he intends to introduce as 'new wine', that his Jewish contemporary Philo, speaking of an intermediary between God and man who would inaugurate a new spiritual life, calls him the 'wine-pourer' and that in the Apocalypse of St John the new Christian era is called the marriage-feast of the Lamb, we begin to see that this 'beginning of signs' as John calls it has a quite fundamental significance: for the water of Judaism our Lord offers the new wine of its successor. We may remark in passing what a prominent part Mary played in this symbol of her son's religion and what a part she plays in it still.

---

[2] John 2:1—4:42.

The second sign, following immediately upon the first without as yet any explanatory discourse, is the expulsion of the buyers and sellers from the Temple. Now the Temple was the standing representative of the old régime with all its sacrificial worship. Whatever the significance given to the event in the Synoptic gospels, John's peculiar quotation from the prophet Zacharias seems to show that he is thinking of the day of the Lord, that is to say the new Messianic age, which the prophet speaks of in that place. In expelling the sellers of doves and the changers of money Jesus is attacking the whole system of Temple worship—for which the business of these merchants was necessary. Indeed, in John our Lord proceeds to promise a substitute for the old Temple, a substitute which is in itself a *semeion,* a sign, (the sign for which the Jews asked), his risen body. 'Destroy this Temple', he says, 'and in three days I will have it up again.' He was speaking of the temple of his body, says John; but the disciples understood only after the Resurrection. Once again, and this time more clearly, John explains, as the Synoptics did not, a sign that all things were to be made new.

Now these two signs, of which the meaning is already beginning to appear, are followed by two discourses, both again turning on the same theme of a new beginning. In the first, our Lord's discourse with Nicodemus, once more the new confronts the old because John is careful to call Nicodemus 'the teacher in Israel'. Our Lord equivalently reads the epitaph of the old order when to the uncomprehending 'teacher in Israel' he declares the necessity of a new birth if the kingdom is to be won. He now takes the symbol of water—giving it a new significance, because symbols are plastic things—for the new régime he intends to introduce, the new creation he intends to perform: 'Unless a man be born of water and the Holy Spirit (as once the world was made when the Spirit hovered over the waters) he cannot enter the kingdom.'

The second discourse is with the Samaritan wom-

an at the well of Jacob. Water is therefore a natural
theme. But there is an explicit contrast between two
kinds of water: there is, first, the very earthly water
of which Jacob and his sons drank—that is to say
the representatives of the Israelite nation—and the
fountain of living water our Lord himself offers.
Here again therefore we might say that the sign of
Cana has been taken up in a new fashion but with
the same profound meaning. The sign of the Temple
recurs here also. The woman asks if it is right to
worship in the Samaritan temple or in Jerusalem.
Our Lord equivalently answers: 'Neither'. The hour
comes, he says, and now is when those who worship
truly will do so in spirit and in truth. In other words,
whatever Temple there is to be will not be confined
to one place. We cannot but remember that he had
spoken of the temple of his body and wonder how
that body can defy the laws of space. But we shall
come to this later.

At the end of this episode therefore we come away
with the impression that a new thing is being brought
to the world by Christ, as superior to the old as wine
to water, spring water to stagnant, temple not built
by hands to man-built temple, a temple chained to
no rock. You will notice that, so far as the ideas
and terms go, there is little here that we could not
find in the other gospels: we remember Matthew's
Sermon on the Mount with its significant opposition:
'It was said to them of old but I say to you'; we remember the Synoptic reference to the new wine in
old bottles and to the wine Jesus drinks with publicans and sinners, we remember the command to bap-
tize with water, we remember the final condemnation on the charge that Jesus claimed to destroy the
Temple. All these things, I say, are there but none
are theologically worked out. They are a proof however that John's intention was certainly not to invent
for his purpose but to take the common deposit and
invest it at theological interest.

With this introduction to the mind of the evangelist we may now come to the great Eucharistic

chapter, John's sixth, of which our Lord's own person is the centre. The sign, the multiplication of the loaves, John has in common with the other evangelists. The discourse is his own. We have seen that the Law, that is the old order, was compared with water; the Rabbis compared it also with bread and, as it seems, with the manna of the desert wandering. We have also seen that our Lord intended to substitute something much superior to the old régime, something which John himself describes as 'grace and truth' as opposed to the Law. Now in the discourse our Lord's opening complaint is that the Jews have followed him not because they had seen signs (John's word is often and unfortunately translated 'miracles') but because they had eaten of the loaves. He reproaches them therefore with not having seen the significance of this bread. He then promises a bread of another sort and like the Samaritan woman who asked him for water, they say: 'Give us always this bread'. His answer takes him infinitely beyond the traditional Jewish expectation of the Messiah; the manna Moses gave did not come truly from heaven, but our Lord does not simply promise to give them bread from heaven—this might only have made him a greater Moses; instead he makes a statement no prophet could have dared to make, a statement that can only have sounded like blasphemy: 'I am the bread from heaven'.

Now at this point we must remember that we are in the gospel of John; we are in a determined theological context; we have to remember that it is the Word, that is to say the Wisdom, of God who is speaking. We have seen that in the fourth gospel Christ offers something in place of the Law, the Torah, which was itself an expression of God's wisdom. Here this 'something' is found to be himself. And indeed in this very chapter our Lord makes it clear that he is speaking as the Wisdom of God. 'He that comes to me shall not hunger; he that believes in me shall not thirst.' These words are a deliberate echo of the words attributed to divine wisdom itself in the book of Ecclesiasticus: 'Those who eat me shall hunger again; those who drink me shall thirst again'. Now this claim of our Lord to be the wisdom of God is not restricted to the first part of the discourse but is found also in what is often called the strictly Eucharistic section.[3] No converted Jew reading John's gospel and already familiar with the invitation uttered by divine wisdom in the book of Proverbs: 'Come, eat my bread and drink the wine I have mixed for you', familiar also with the ancient Christian formula: 'This bread my body, this wine my blood', no such Jew could miss the reference when our Lord says: 'Except you eat the flesh of the Son of Man and drink his blood, you shall not have life in you'. The reader would know very well that this 'Son of Man' was identifying himself with the wisdom of God. In the sixth chapter of St John, therefore, our Lord is asking for unconditional surrender of mind and heart and person to him. St John calls this 'receiving' him, a verb which in the Synoptic gospels might be translated 'welcome' in the social sense ('He that receives you receives me') but which in John assumes explicitly the depth that the other gospels leave it to ourselves to sound.

But do not misunderstand. I am far from saying that the Eucharistic discourse is an appeal for trustful faith without any sacramental reference. No doubt the Church leaves us free to follow this opinion, which was that of Origen and of Clement of Alexandria, but the whole historical context is against it. When the fourth gospel was written, the Eucharistic ceremony was the central rite of the rapidly expanding Christian society, and had been for more than fifty years. No Christian reader could possibly miss the reference to this repetition of the Last Supper. Indeed it has been said that this very chapter is John's way of bringing in the Last Supper with its Eucharistic institution, left out by him in that place. But all this must not be allowed to obscure what, one feels, is a certain fact, namely that throughout this

[3] John 6:51-59.

discourse our Lord is speaking precisely as the Word or Wisdom of God. If we remember this, the long-standing difficulty of the unexpectedness of the nine specifically sacramental verses in a discourse on faith disappears. The unity of the discourse is preserved because its whole theme is seen to be union, union with Christ the Word and the Wisdom. The appeal of the whole chapter is for acceptance of the Word, the creative and redeeming Wisdom of God. But the peak of this acceptance is reached in personal commitment to the efficacy of our Lord's redeeming death (which is already broadly hinted at in the separate mention of body and blood: 'eat my flesh, drink my blood', as also in the phrase 'my flesh [given] for the life of the world'). By this we are united to the Crucified. Now this union is expressed most directly and achieved efficaciously by sacramental means. One might venture to say, always subject to the Church's judgment, that the theme of John 6 is throughout union by faith with our Lord's efficacious Passion and Resurrection, a faith of which the outward, perfect, operative expression is the reception of the Holy Eucharist.

There is one other aspect of St John's gospel that we cannot omit. It has a connection too, with what we have said so far. I am referring to John's conception of the relationship between what the Rabbis called, and the Synoptic gospels also, with a shift of sense, 'this age' and 'the age to come'. When we read the Synoptic gospels we feel that our attention is being directed primarily, though not exclusively, to the future and to the glorious 'return' of Christ at what we call the end of time. St John does not lose sight of this time-element but he brings out clearly the fact that eternity has entered time, as it were; this different dimension (I call it a dimension because eternity is not simply a long time but a timeless modality of existence) now pervades time like an atmosphere. His formula is very revealing: 'The time is coming and now is', a paradoxical expression neatly bringing out what we have called the entrance of another dimension. 'The time is coming, and now is, when the dead shall hear the voice of the Son of God'—our Lord is not speaking here, as in a later verse, of the emergence of the dead from the tombs; he is referring to events in the spiritual world within this world of ours. The explanation of this different emphasis in John is that he is the evangelist of the Word made flesh, a flesh to be 'received' by all who wish. For John the whole human world has become sacramental—the outward sign which is the Word made flesh communicates here and now the inward grace of the Word himself. He is saying that even now the world is a different place; what it will become is almost secondary. It is what we mean when we say that grace and glory are the same thing with the accidental difference of the passing of time and the coming of death.

The period to which John is referring is, of course, the time of his writing, the time after Resurrection and Ascension, what we sometimes rather misleadingly call the Age of the Spirit. With this period John himself expressly contrasts the time before our Lord's Ascension: 'The Spirit was not yet given', he says, 'because Jesus was not yet glorified'. This observation leads us perhaps to an understanding of one of the most difficult sentences in John. When our Lord meets the Magdalen in the garden after his Resurrection he says: 'Do not keep on handling me because I have not yet ascended to my Father'. The words themselves suggest a reference to the sentence we have just quoted. The implication of our Lord's words to Mary seems to be that he may be freely 'handled' after the Ascension. Taking our two texts together, it looks as if we are here in presence of John's sacramental thesis. The body of Christ communicates the Spirit but only, as a fixed and general rule, after this body has become suffused with the Spirit—I mean with Spirit as communicable—after the Ascension, that is to say the final glorification when the body 'sits at the right hand of the Father', which is the Christian picturesque expression for the ultimate consecration of the body of Christ. After this entrance into, assumption of, heavenly glory familiar contact may begin. What kind of contact? Sacramental contact. To establish this we must invoke various texts of John. We have already called attention to a key text in this matter: 'The Spirit was not yet given because Jesus was not yet glorified'. This glorification was achieved by the Resurrection and the return to the Father: 'If I do not leave you', says our Lord, 'the Paraclete will not come to you'. Jesus possessed the Spirit before, because the Word was God, says John; and his glory was no new thing: 'Glorify your Son', our Lord prays, 'with the glory I had with you before the world was made'. But this was a pre-incarnate glory; the difference now is that the body of Christ is glorified, suffused with the Spirit, diffusing the Spirit. The Ascension of our Lord's body is therefore the condition of the sacramental system. And more specifically it is connected with the Eucharist. In the sixth chapter of which we have spoken our Lord deliberately refers to his Ascension: 'Is this a stumbling block to you?', he asks, speaking of his Eucharistic doctrine; 'what if you see the Son of Man ascending to where he was before?' We may conjecture that this remark was meant to put his hearers on the right track, to realize the enormous powers of such a body. He then goes on immediately to say: 'It is the Spirit that gives life, the flesh is powerless'. It is natural to conclude from all these texts that by the Ascension the body of Christ took possession of that glorified state that enabled him to dispense that body, particularly under a Eucharistic form.

The body of Christ is therefore from now and for ever the centre of worship by which we enter into the presence of God; it is absolved for ever from the old limitations of space and time; it is to be found not only on this mountain nor on that; through it we receive the Spirit of God and the Word of God; we worship 'in spirit and in truth'.

CHAPTER 9

The Word
between the Testaments

IT is not for the Catholic mind, that takes so naturally to the idea of living tradition, to ignore the voice of the Jewish tradition before Christ.[1] The Spirit assuredly did not cease to guide the nation that produced Zachary, Elizabeth, Mary herself— the 'poor of God', outstanding surely but not isolated. The hiatus between the Biblical economies is therefore literary and canonical only; between the economies themselves there is no rupture. But if there are traces of this continuity it behooves us to study them. We are speaking of the light certain new discoveries throw not on the Biblical text [2] but on the religious mind, or one corner of it, with which our Lord with his precursor and his followers had to do. They are a thin shaft of brightness falling on some part of the cradle of the Word made flesh. We welcome it, for the dichotomy is false that is implied in a recent popular book on our subject, namely that 'the rise of Christianity should at last be generally understood as an episode in human history rather than propagated as dogma and divine revelation'.[3] The supernatural and the historical are not two incompatibles, though they be incommensurables; even Incarnation, assumption of a finite nature by an Infinite, cannot exhaust the Word of God to man, but

[1] And after, too, no doubt. But this is another and more difficult question.

[2] Though indeed they begin to make a history of the Old Testament text appear at last possible.

[3] E. Wilson, *The Scrolls from the Dead Sea* (New York, 1955), p. 108.

the Catholic at least holds it to be a divine intervention in history. The Word was made flesh: history is revelation.

When documents can fetch as much as three pounds sterling per square inch it may be supposed that they are not uninteresting. These we speak of are associated with Khirbet Qumran, the ruined remains of the headquarters of that semi-monastic, semi-eremitical body of priestly penitents known as the Community of the Alliance. For our purpose it is precise enough to say that they occupied the site and the caves in its neighbourhood from the end of the second century B.C. to the first A.D., finally deserting it when the Tenth Legion marched on Jericho on its way to the siege of Jerusalem (A.D. 67).

All the world knows of the 1947 discovery (Cave 1). The hunt was up, and some are still scouring the rock-face west of the Dead Sea. Their most rewarding find was that of Cave 4 in September, 1952. This mass of new material forced the recruitment of a small team of scholars who carried on with their work conscious of the popular impatience but fortunately not disturbed by it. More than once Père de Vaux, director of the investigation, had to protect his team by protesting that it was not yet the time for syntheses—still less for popularizations.[4]

In these circumstances it is premature to offer appraisals that claim to be complete and final. It is true that even angels have not feared to tread this insufficiently charted ground, but the venture has not been entirely without damage. The brilliant intuitions even of a Dupont-Sommer were set down side by side with too bold a portrait of the Teacher of Righteousness, founder of the sect, in terms of the Christian belief and hope.[5] The author later ad-

---

[4] *Revue Biblique*, 1953, p. 625; 1955, p. 632.

[5] *Aperçus préliminaires sur les manuscripts de la Mer Morte*, Paris, 1950. The teacher was said to have been regarded as a divine being incarnate; he was a redeemer put to death and his second coming was expected.

mitted that this was 'a parallel hastily drawn to prick
the curiosity of his readers'.[6] In our own country,
an excellent series of talks was somewhat marred by
similar suggestions which, though offered as such,
were likely to mislead an uncritical public.[7] Granted
that the niceties of scholarly debate are not for the
uninstructed ear, it still remains our duty to indicate
the dissent of other scholars when it exists. Thus
the reading of the Habacuc commentary which is
said to refer to the violent death of the Teacher is
very much disputed. In the same way it might be
wise to await the publication of other editions of the
Community's famous *Manual of Discipline,* now being studied, before we draw firm conclusions from
the one edition available. And, as for the ready intervention of the unqualified, one can only apply to
this the severe but just verdict—or epitaph—earned
by the French popular journals: 'The Press is no
longer interested and it would be better if it never
had been.' [8]

But though temerity is blameworthy, its dangerous
opposite which is indifference or inertia is also to be
discouraged. The development of the Word is always of importance. Even if the development be at
times distortion, this too may serve to enlighten by

[6] *Nouveaux aperçus* . . . , Paris, 1953, p. 207.

[7] Mr. John M. Allegro in the Northern Home Service Radio
programme, 16, 23 and 30 January, 1956, at 7:15 p.m. Mr.
Allegro is assistant lecturer in Comparative Semitic Philology
at Manchester University. He became a member of the team of
scholars working at the Rockefeller Museum, Jordan, in Octo-
ber, 1953. Other members of the team dissociated themselves
at least from certain impressions produced by the talks in a
letter to *The Times,* 16 March 1956. In his reply in the same
newspaper a few days later the speaker called attention to the
tentative nature of his reconstruction. He had said that in all
probability the Teacher had been handed over to the gentiles to
be crucified, and carefully taken down from his cross; the body
was lovingly watched over by his disciples in the expectation
of its resurrection. The speaker's terms had been chosen to match
those of the Gospels.

[8] J. Delorme in *L' Ami du Clergé,* 1955, p. 656.

contrast the teaching of the Word himself made flesh.
Now infant Christianity and Qumran had this first
thing in common, that they were two spiritual com-
munities, existing together in time and not far distant in place, each of which was cut off from the
body of official Judaism. It is indeed a symptom of
their deep difference that while this official Judaism
had resisted advances from Christianity it had been
itself deserted by Qumran; nevertheless, each would
understand the other when it addressed Pharisees
and Sadducees as a 'brood of vipers'. But Christianity's confrontation was Qumran's withdrawal. For
lack of more offensive weapons the 'sons of Sadoq'—
the leaders claimed physical descent — chose this
form of protest against a usurped high-priesthood.
For them the Maccabean movement had gone wrong:
the holy war against Syrian Hellenism had not restored the legitimate Sadoqite priesthood. From the
time of Jonathan (161-143 B.C.), brother of Judas
Maccabeus, the high office had remained in the Maccabean family. What remained for the sons of Sadoq?
Retirement in hope that God would reassert the ancient right. So they withdrew, taking as their interim
charter—as Christianity was later to do—the words
of the Book of Consolation (Is 40:3): 'Prepare in
the wilderness the way of our God'.

In what did the preparation consist? Not in war-
like exercise. It seems true to say that the Qumran
sect was not pacifist as the Jehovah's Witness are not
pacifist,[9] though when we read its 'War' scroll (or
'Fighter's Manual') we must bear in mind Dodd's
warning on the interpretation of the eschatological
combats in Ezechiel and Daniel.[10] The military dis-

[9] Bruce, *New Testament Studies*, 2, 1956, p. 188, quotes the
reported statement of the international leader of the Witnesses
at Twickenham in August of 1955; 'they were conscientious objectors in relation to wars of the present order, they were not
absolute pacifists; they believed in a war—the eschatological
warfare of Armageddon.'

[10] C. H. Dodd, *According to the Scriptures* (London, 1952),
p. 73: 'We shall be wise to treat the entire scheme of imagery

positions are minute and, it is said, modelled on the Roman technique; but on the other hand there is a ritual character attaching to them [11] which suggests unreality. But this at least should be said, that the 'War' scroll is a most bitter expression of hatred for all that is not Jewish and a blueprint for vengeance. We are very far from Christianity. 'Jesus could, no doubt, have launched a holy war, and would have found many enthusiastic followers had he done so. But it is as certain as anything can be that he rejected the whole conception of such a warfare— whether in the immediate Zealot form or in the deferred Qumran form—in favour of the way of the Suffering Servant.' [12] The war of our Apocalypse (e.g. 20:7 ff) is not against flesh and blood; nor is there even in the known Jewish literature anything to match the fierce attacks upon individuals, unnamed but recognizable, that we find in Qumran's commentary on Habacuc.[13]

This for our sense of proportion. But let us see the reverse of the coin. Abstention from the official cult, though only a temporary measure, promoted a detached and more thoughtful spirituality. The first line of the *Manual of Discipline* firmly lays down St Benedict's rule. 'To seek God.' Needless to say, whoever enters the Community takes oath 'to devote himself to the Law of Moses . . . as it has been revealed to the sons of Sadoq' and 'as revealed from time to time and as the Prophets have revealed it through the Holy Spirit', but these qualifications in themselves and in their historical situation prepare us for a more generous interpretation than that of the

as language appropriate to describe that which lies upon the frontier of normal experience, which therefore cannot be directly communicated by plain speech.'

[11] *Nouvelle Revue Théologique*, 1955, pp. 372-99.

[12] *New Testament Studies, loc. cit.*

[13] *Biblica*, 1954, p. 343.

Pharisees and for a different emphasis.[14] In fact they
made way for the 'mercy and not sacrifice' theme of
the Prophets [15] and enabled a metaphorical interpretation of the Mosaic sacrificial system. In place of
that system stood the careful observance of the Community's rules which, under the good pleasure of
God, would expiate sin. For consciousness of guilt
is not the least admirable nor the least Christian
quality of Qumran which regarded itself as a home
of penitents. Such a reaction from the insouciance
of the Sadducees and self-sufficiency of Pharisaism
inevitably brought with it a total personal commital
to the divine mercy, a higher perception of what we
call 'grace'. In these circumstances it seems to us
unjust to accuse the sect of a Calvinistic predestina-
tion doctrine: the emphasis on God's *dominium* has
provoked the same accusation at more advanced
stages of theology, and still unjustly; in a time and
milieu where speculation was not acceptable and
formulas unmade, the accusation is an anachron-
ism. As in the New Testament itself the two data
of divine choice and human effort appear side by
side without a reconciling philosophy; may it be that
human experience in prayer as in effort can do without one? And so, if we may resume, in place of the
sacrificial vocabulary we find recurring at Qumran
the words 'truth, humility, justice, love of goodness,
mercy'. We can guess at our Lord's approval, who
once said to the Pharisees: 'You have left the weight-
ier things of the Law: justice and mercy and faith'
(Mt 23:23).

The concluding Blessing of the *Discipline Manual*,
reminiscent of the *Benedictus* of Zachary the Sadoqite, father of the Baptist,[16] well expresses the substantial piety of Qumran: 'Blessed be Thou, my God,

---

[14] Owing, doubtless, to its withdrawal from the Temple, Qumran seems at times to pass beyond the salutary emphasis of the
Prophets almost to a condemnation of sacrifice.

[15] Amos 5:24; Os 6:6; Is 1:11-17; Mich 6:6-8.

[16] *Revue Biblique*, 1955, pp. 41-2.

who throwest wide the heart of Thy servant to receive knowledge. . . .[17] Grant to the son of Thy
handmaid to stand before Thee for ever. For without Thee no way is perfect: without Thy good pleasure nothing can be done.'

Here at Qumran we have a notable preparation of
heart for a worship in spirit and in truth, centred not
on this mountain nor on that: for a religion Jewish
in its origins which could yet survive, even thrive
upon, the destruction of the Holy City itself. Such a
revelation was Qumran to the few. Theirs was the
lesson the Babylonian exile had read to many. And
yet the Community maintained a shadow hierarchy
ready to take over in the great day of the Visit, of
the divine rescue and renewal of Jerusalem, when-
ever it should come. The true perspective of the
Temple was not permanently achieved. Christianity
on the other hand seems to have grasped it firmly
from its earliest days and so stood braced for uni-
versality. Already in the thirties of the first century
Stephen puts the Temple in its due place (Acts 7:44-
50); his confidence was surely based upon deduc-
tion from the words of Jesus (e.g., Mark 14:58; cf.
John 2:19-21). Temple, priesthood and sacrifice
were all and already gathered into one in the person
of Christ. On this point as on others it is the intervention of that person in history which reveals the
gulf (though it offers the bridge, too), between Christianity and Qumran.

By the very force of their origins, therefore, the
sectaries were sharply aware of an unfaithful Israel
that had compromised with paganism. From this
Israel they had seceded and their secession had
drawn a clear line between two camps. To use their

[17] 'When *da'at*, "knowledge", and related terms appear in
the *Manual of Discipline*, it is seldom a question of knowledge
in the modern, intellectual, sense of the word. And the underlying idea is scarcely ever to be identified with the more abstract
"gnosis" of Gnosticism' (Bo Reicke in *New Testament Studies*,
I. 1954, p. 138). Here it is acknowledgment and performance
of God's will.

own expression: 'the sons of light' had withdrawn from 'the sons of darkness'. These two were not yet at grips, nor would be until the eschatological combat was engaged. Rather, the present duty of the sons of light was to refuse all contaminating contact: not one of them would have sat down to eat with Simon the Pharisee. Nevertheless, the 'spirit of lies' which [18] directed the camp of darkness could and did pass into the camp of light, contending for mastery in the heart of each member whose destiny turned upon the issue. In this struggle, despite expressions suggesting a fatality in the distribution of the opposing spirit to each man, it seems clear that human free-will is truly in action.

The 'sons of light or darkness' terminology is not without parallel even in the Synoptic gospels (Luke 16:8) and of itself is perhaps a natural enough Hebraism [19] though not found in the Old Testament. But the persistence and pervasion of the light-dark motif is noticeable in both the Scrolls and the Johannine literature, and this emphasis is impressive. There is at least a common background of thought and of expression. In many cases of likeness between the Qumran literature and the New Testament, appeal may legitimately be made to the Old Testament as a common source. This is scarcely possible here. The dualism [20] implied in the light-dark opposition and expressed by the doctrine of the two spirits is foreign to the Old Testament and indeed to indigenous Hebrew thought. Infiltration from the uncompromising dualism of Zoroastrianism is not unlikely [21]; through the further filter of the Qumran school of thought it may have passed to St John's gospel and first epistle. In this, as in many other respects, the fourth

[18] Or 'who'. It appears so far impossible to decide whether the 'spirits' are persons or motive-powers.

[19] This view is argued by G. Graystone in *Irish Theological Quarterly*, 1956, p. 33.

[20] The dualism of Qumran is of course modified: the two 'spirits' are created and controlled by the one God.

[21] Cf. *Catholic Biblical Quarterly*, 1955, pp. 405 ff.

gospel may begin to display evidence of more Jewish contacts than many critics have been willing to concede.

But it is the style of the edifice rather than the choice of quarry that distinguishes an author's thought. We have said that Qumran was a withdrawal, Christianity a confrontation; because while the one lived on expectation the other was confident it had received. For our Essene sect [22] light and darkness pursued their parallel courses and the combat was reserved for the future. For St John—and this is the nerve of the matter—light and dark had already engaged decisively: and the light shone in the darkness and the darkness did not master it. The prince of this world (the *Mastema* of Qumran, the equivalent *Satan* of John) was already cast out, already judged. In such terms Jesus saluted the hour of his crucifixion, the hour of his triumph. Qumran could say 'the hour cometh', but John could add 'and now is'.

With their hope for a happy future this 'Community of the Alliance' connected the manifestation of a messianic figure. In this they are in line with the Prophets. But in the days of the monarchy the hope had naturally been associated with the dynasty; after the Exile when a high priest replaced the Davidic king the same hope, equally naturally, attached to the priesthood also. Thus in Zacharias (4:1-14: 519 B.C.) Josue the Sadoqite priest and Zorobabel the Davidic prince stand together as portents of the messianic age. Subsequently the emphasis changes: royal messianism recedes, though it does not disappear; sacerdotal messianism comes to the fore. Thus Ecclesiasticus (45:6-24; c. 190 B.C.) stresses the priestly hope, and an apparently contemporary hand has substituted Josue the priest for Zorobabel in Zacharias 6:11. But the Davidic and the Sadoqite Messiahs both appear (the Davidic first) in the

[22] That Qumran was the Essene foundation is an opinion gaining in favour.

psalm the Hebrew text of Ecclesiasticus inserts between Ecclus. 51:12 and 51:13.[23]

Against this background we must read the hope of Qumran. For it seems established [24] that there also two Messiahs were expected to manifest themselves in the latter days: 'the Priest' and 'the Messiah of Israel'. In that priestly community it is not surprising that the Sadoqite 'Priest' takes precedence over the 'Messiah of Israel', a layman. He is to preside at the banquet at the end of times and sing the praises of the victories won by the Messiah of Israel over the camp of darkness. The Sadoqite and Davidic hopes, therefore, coexist though the Davidic is subordinate.[25]

While the messianism of Qumran remained in suspense, Christianity, though it too looked forward, was convinced that it had already reached the endtime. In the New Testament, moreover, the variegated strands of the messianic hope are found woven into one tapestry. The Son of David, Son of Man, Suffering Servant expiating sin [26] are all identified in one person, gathered into a powerful synthesis initiated by an embracing and creative mind.[27] But one problem still remained: the priesthood of a Davidic Messiah. For its own part Qumran could not suggest that Priest and King might be united in one figure—Levitical and Judan origin were clearly irrecon-

[23] Cf. *Bible de Jérusalem*, note ad loc.

[24] This interpretation, originally proposed by Fr. J. T. Milik in *Verbum Domini*, 1951, p. 152 and cf. *Revue Biblique*, 1953, pp. 290-2, is gaining acceptance; cf. Kuhn in *New Testament Studies*, I. 1955, pp. 168-79.

[25] It is unfortunate that the third Isaiah commentary, apropos Is 10:22-11:4, expressly mentioning a Davidic Messiah, is torn. The MS is one of Mr. Allegro's group. He mentions that the tear is new and that there is hope of recovering the remainder; cf. *Revue Biblique*, 1956, p. 62.

[26] The notion of expiation by the few on behalf of the many is found in the *Manual of Discipline* (cf. 8:6-10; 9:4).

[27] Cf. Dodd, *According to the Scriptures*, p. 109; the creative mind is our Lord's.

cilable. It is to this question that the inspired author of the *Epistle to the Hebrews* addresses himself. He dissolves the duality of Qumran's messianic hope by claiming for our Lord a priesthood 'after the fashion of Melchisedech'. By a method of argument calculated to appeal to those familiar with the verbal ingenuity of *midrash* interpretation, he demonstrates the superiority of that pre-Mosaic priesthood over the priesthood of Levi and so of Sadoq (Heb. 7:1-19). There is no dilemma therefore; Jesus of Juda cannot be a Levitical priest, but he enjoys an office that is not tribal; it is universal and not less but more from God, for indeed 'the Law could not achieve what is perfect'.[28]

That the New Testament must be appraised as controversy before it is assessed as history is no doubt a statement to be greeted with caution, but it must at least be recalled that the inspired authors wrote for a public which had its own interests and difficulties. In this matter of the priestly Messiah we have an example which, maybe, is close to our subject. It is worthy of notice that *Hebrews* by insisting upon the Aaronic priesthood is, equally with the Qumran sect, hostile to the non-Aaronic Sadducees who were in possession: 'No one', says the Epistle, 'must take this dignity to himself: he must be called by God, precisely as Aaron was' (5:4). But this very principle would seem to oppose Qumran to the priesthood of Jesus of Juda. Hence the manifest anxiety of the author to deal with the difficulty. Is it too bold to suppose that he had the Sectaries in mind? It is in the first place inconceivable that the early Christian preachers should ignore the truly spiritual aspirations and difficulties of this *élite* of Israel, provided they were in touch with it. That they did meet is surely probable. It is known that there were pockets of Essene members or sympathizers in every town of Palestine, ancestors of Qumran itself had migrated as far afield as Damascus forty years after the death

28 Cf. *Revue Biblique*, 1955, pp. 35-37.

of the Teacher of Righteousness [29]; in Ephesus supporters of the Baptist, and therefore presumably acquainted with Qumran, were installed (Acts 19: 1-4). Christian contact with such groups would go far towards explaining not only the background of the Epistle to the Hebrews, but also the indications of relationship between Qumran and the Johannine literature, possibly even the less certain affinity of phrases in the Pauline epistles.[30]

Relative to this question of messianism is the use the New Testament makes of the Old Testament. Rendel Harris's theory of a pre-New Testament volume of 'Testimonies' may appear extravagant [31] but the evidence of the New Testament texts at least demands lesser florilegia [32] with which Christianity could illustrate its continuity with Israel and the unity of the divine plan. Qumran now offers support. One of the documents of Mr. Allegro's group [33] is an anthology of messianic passages from Exodus, 2 Samuel, Isaiah, Amos, Psalms, Daniel. A leaf from Cave 4 lists Deut 18:18-19 ('I will raise them up a prophet,' etc.) with Num 24:15-17 ('A star shall rise out of Jacob,' etc.) and Deut 33:8-11 ('Thy perfection and Thy doctrine—shall be—with Thy holy one'). Of these three texts the first is used in the earliest days of Christianity (Acts 3:22 f). The

[29] If the preacher is to be identified with the high priest Onias III, he died in 171 B.C. But perhaps more probably he was a personality of Alexander Jannaeus's reign (103-76 B.C.), or possibly even of the Pompeyan period (c. 67 B.C.). The identification of the sect with the Ebionites and of the Teacher with Our Lord himself is no longer possible: the evidence that the Community was in existence several decades before Christ is now conclusive. Nor was the Teacher regarded as Messiah in the strict sense.

[30] On this last cf. W. Grossouw, *Studia Catholica*, 1952, pp. 1-5; S. E. Johnson, *Harvard Theological Review*, 1955, pp. 157-65.

[31] Dodd, *loc. cit.*, pp. 23-7.

[32] Cerfaux, *Recueil Lucien Cerfaux*, 1954, vol. 2, p. 226.

[33] *Revue Biblique*, 1956, p. 63.

second though not found in the New Testament, is
used by Justin Martyr in the second century and
doubtless lies behind the Star incident in St Matthew's account of the Infancy. The well-known
'Stone' cycle of applications deriving from the 'precious cornerstone' of Isaiah 28:16 [34] is also repre-
sented in Qumran. There the trusty stone is identified with the council of the Community.[35] For the
early Christians the stone is our Lord himself (I
Peter 2:6: cf. Rom 9:33) and Peter the Rock shares
his quality (Mt 16:18); but Qumran's collective interpretation is found also: those united with Christ
are themselves living stones built into a mystical
temple (Eph 2:20 ff; I Peter 2:5).[36]

The remains of an elaborate water system with its
great stepped cisterns are tangible witnesses to the
references to purification in the *Manual of Discipline*.
It appears that these baths were not a ceremony of
initiation but rather a privilege of tried members:
moral purity had first to be proved before admission
to the purifications was conceded. It is therefore
difficult to decide the part these played in the process of sanctification, but unlike the usual Jewish purifications they seem to have enjoyed a certain efficacy
in relation to sin. The stain of guilt affected even

34 Cf. V. Taylor, *The Names of Jesus*, 1954, pp. 93-9.

35 Cf. *Zeitschrift f.d. A. T. Wissenschaft*, 1954, p. 113.

36 There is similarity, too, in the method of O. T. exegesis
which is neither Rabbinic nor allegorical. The reason is that
both the sectaries and the Christians considered that they lived
at the end of times: for Christianity the time had come, for
Qumran it was imminent. Consequently the O. T. is taken up
and applied in each to the present time. Nevertheless, exag-
geration in this matter must be avoided. Thus both Qumran
and N. T. (Rom 1:17; Gal 3: 11; Heb 10:37 ff.) take up Hab
2:4 which speaks of *fidelity* to God's will. Qumran applies the
text to the Teacher, N. T. to our Lord. But the perspectives differ: the Teacher is not an object of faith for Qumran as Christ
is for Christianity. We should therefore understand, against
Dupont-Sommer, 'loyalty to the teaching of the Teacher' rather
than faith in him as redeemer. Cf. S. E. Johnson, *loc. cit.*,
p. 165.

the body; it must be progressively removed day by day until the final messianic purification by the spirit of holiness—the definitive messianic baptism.[37]

As Josephus describes it the baptism of John is scarcely distinguishable from any purification at Qumran: John's baptism was administered 'with the purification of the body in view once the soul had been purified by justness'. But Josephus had not the whole story; the gospels are more fully informed and the highlight of their portrait is the prophetic and urgent nature of John's mission. While at Qumran the devout community of pious scribes laboured to prepare for the time of the Visit, applying to themselves the Isaian text: 'In the desert prepare the way of the Lord', and adding, 'this "way" is the study of the Law', a few miles away the Baptist was crying: 'The axe is even now laid to the root'. For that reason his baptism was not a series of purifications but an urgent, final, unique ceremony. For him there was no preparatory term of probation; there was no time to waste, humble acceptance of his baptism was part of the act of conversion itself. John was no patient scribe, he was a resolute prophet with a sure sense that his vocation pressed, conscious that his own 'manifestation' was a sign of the imminence of Judgment. Nor was his baptism for a tried *élite:* even the Sadducees, who would have had short thrift from Qumran, were welcome if in truth they feared the coming wrath. And it would have shocked the sectaries to hear John ordering his baptized soldiers and publicans back to their work with all its pagan contaminations. Moreover the Baptist aimed at the purification of a whole people for the Messiah's coming, a national appeal perhaps, but not confined to the sons of Abraham, for God could raise such from the stones. If we speak of 'baptism' in relation to Qumran and to St John the Baptist, we should do well to recall the distance between the self-performed, recurrent, leisurely nature of the one and

[37] On all this cf. *Lumière et Vie*, March, 1956, p. 254.

the unique, urgent character of the other that John himself administered in the full consciousness of his individual, personal mission. The rite remains, its significance has changed.[38]

The early Christians, like the Qumran community, looked upon themselves as the faithful remnant of the true Israel. Both movements claimed the same titles: 'the elect of God', 'the poor ones', 'those of the Way', and pledged their loyalty to a 'new Alliance'. [39] Both met periodically for their sacred meal, a rehearsal of the great messianic banquet in the latter days. At Qumran only the fully fledged members — the *Rabbim* — partook. Seniority was carefully regulated: presiding priest, priests according to age, layfolk. Though possibly unjust to the pursuit of humility at Qumran, it is difficult not to recall our Lord's 'Be not called *rabbi* (Mt 23:8) and the competition for precedence at the Last Supper (Luke 22:24-7) which Jesus shamed by his own startling example (John 13:4-16). The president then blessed and divided the bread and the wine and each at table proceeded to do the same in turn. Here, therefore, we have a sacred meal in which bread and wine are prominent, with rules laid down for their blessing. The analogy with the Last Supper is unmistakable though in one important respect it breaks down: not the president only but each at table takes and blesses his own food. This ritual and sacred ceremony at Qumran emphasized the com-

---

[38] John's seemingly self-contradictory phrase foretelling Christ's baptism 'in the Holy Spirit and in fire' (sanctification as opposed to condemnation) get some light from the *Manual* which compares the spirit not only with cleansing water but also with a purifying furnace. Hence though the 'fire' of the Baptism is indeed a fire of judgment (Mt. 3: 10-12), it may also include the idea of purification.

[39] But here again we must set a phrase in its historical context: Qumran's application to the Law together with the nature of its hopes for the fuure invite us to think rather of a renewed than a new Alliance.

mon fellowship of the society, the communion of the priest with others and of others together.

With the evidence of this thoroughly Jewish community before our eyes the thesis becomes more than ever untenable that St Paul under pagan influence introduced a ritual character into our Lord's last meal with his disciples which was in fact commonplace in all except that it was his last. An unritual primitive Christianity is a mirage.[40] But whereas the fathers had eaten manna in the desert, and in the desert the Community of the Alliance celebrated its rite of bread and wine, the ceremony of the Upper Room was endowed with an entirely new significance. The disciples there were united with the priestly Messiah presiding at the table, sacramentally gathered into that Body which was to die and rise. Here again it is the historical intervention of Christ's person that marks Christianity off from Qumran.[41] It is true that for Christian disciples, as for the Community the Meal is a rehearsal of the great messianic banquet where many shall sit down with Abraham in the Kingdom: and it is true that though the Resurrection of Christ be achieved in fact and of the disciples in principle—by reason of union with the Body—the Christian's manifest resurrection awaits the future [42]: the union is maintained, sacramentally 'until he

[40] Cf. Bouyer, *La Bible et l'Evangile*, 1953, pp. 255-7.

[41] Whether any light is thrown by Qumran on the date of the Last Supper is open to question. The Community preferred the solar calendar to the lunar reckoning of the official clergy. For them 'the sun is the measure of the world'—a statement which might have something to do with the absurd allegation of sun-worship among the Essenes. An attempt on these lines has been made to solve the famous Johannine versus Synoptic controversy: our Lord may have followed the solar calendar of Qumran, the official priesthood the lunar calculation. It has been suggested that the Last Supper may therefore have occurred on Tuesday, cf. A. Jaubert, *Revue de l'Histoire des Religions*, 1954, pp. 140-73. The suggestion perhaps raises more difficulties than it solves.

[42] On the paradoxical intermingling of present and future in the Christian message *cf. Revue Biblique*, 1955, pp. 9-11.

come'. Yet in the mind of Christ and of his disciples all is already consummated.

This is not Qumran but, once granted the Christ-event, Qumran might feel its appeal. Nor would the Community be surprised by the sacrificial atmosphere of the Last Supper.[43] Voluntary exiles from the Temple sacrifice, they seem to have regarded their ritual meals as a substitute,[44] as an official and communal act analogously sacrificial like their whole devotional life which was 'a sacrifice of praise'. This would explain the statement Josephus makes of the Essenes: that while refusing to enter the Temple they offered their own sacrifice at home.[45]

Israel's tradition looked back upon the Exodus as upon the idyllic time of honeymoon: in the first days of their union God had taken Israel into the desert and spoken to her heart. The 'spirituality of the desert' is a legacy of this tradition. And so it was that the monks of Qumran sought God in the desert of Juda; in the same desert our Lord outfaced the tempter; to the same desert St John the Baptist withdrew from his home in 'a city of Juda', preparing for his manifestation to Israel. It seems impossible that John should have known nothing of the great monastery on the bare plateau by the Dead Sea; most unlikely that he was unacquainted with its practices and its hopes. Nor is it extravagant to conjecture that he sought conversation with—even advice from—hermits older than himself.[46]

[43] Cf. J. Jeremias, *The Eucharistic Words of Jesus*, Oxford, 1955, pp. 142-52.

[44] Thus G. Vermès, *Les Manuscrits du Désert de Juda*, 1954, p. 61.

[45] Bones of sheep, lambs, etc. have been discovered on the Khirbet Qumran site, carefully stord in jars. 'They are certainly the remains of sacred meals celebrated by the community. This discovery is of great importance. Its explanation is evidently to be found in religious ordinances of which no trace has yet been found in the documents.' Père de Vaux in *Revue Biblique*, 1956, p. 74.

[46] In A.D. 54 Josephus Flavius, then aged sixteen, went to stay with an Essene hermit and remained for three years.

But that these probabilities are confirmed by the New Testament evidence seems to us difficult to prove. John's invitation to repentance, his threat of vengeance and of lasting fire, these are echoed in the Qumran literature but we confess to finding the similarities not striking. As for his baptismal rite, the practice of baptizing proselytes to Judaism existed demonstrably in the first century A.D. and probably earlier. These baptisms may have been John's model.[47] And even if such baptisms were not at that time tolerated as substitutes for circumcision, fully initiating the proselyte into the Jewish community, they were at least documents of separation from old pagan ways—evidence of a *metanoi,* or change of heart, such as the Baptist demanded. On this as on other points it may be prudent to beware lest the *éclat* of the new discoveries make us forget that if Qumran is a branch of Essenism, Essenism itself is part of a wider tradition upon which the Baptist may independently have drawn. In its final, and, we may say, its initiatory character his baptism is nearer to proselyte baptism than it is to the practice of Qumran.

Perhaps the strongest argument for the Baptist's familiarity with the sect in its headquarters at Qumran is an indirect one. It is considered reasonably certain that St John the evangelist was the Baptist's disciple (cf. John 1:35-40). Now we have remarked the affinities of the fourth gospel with the light and darkness theme which is so characteristic of the Community. It is possible, therefore, that the Baptist's young disciple, instructed in this outlook upon the spiritual world, came to see his divine master's career in those terms. It may be so. But on the other hand the explanation offered above for a similar

[47] Cf. O. Cullmann, *Baptism in the New Testament* (London, 1954), p. 9: 'Judaism already knows of the baptism of proselytes coming over from heathenism. John the Baptist holds all Jews to be like proselytes and demands a baptism to forgiveness of sins from them all, in view of the impending appearance of the Messiah.'

phenomenon in the Epistle to the Hebrews may be sufficient to account for the viewpoint of the Johannine literature also. It is worthy of note, in any case, that we have here one more piece of evidence of authentically Jewish contact in a gospel which was once thought to be so exclusively Greek.

The conditions Qumran sought ultimately to change, Christianity engaged to work with. Our Lord said: 'Render to Caesar' and, of the Pharisees 'what they say to you observe' (Mt 22:21; 23:3). Nor was the break with the Sadducean priesthood of his making, though when that priesthood presided over his condemnation Qumran must have felt a sympathy which might later blossom into acceptance. As for the meeting of minds, there was surely opportunity. For several years Christianity was Palestinian and the break with Judaism gradual: even in the second century Justin the Christian and Trypho the Jew could carry on a measured discussion. In the same century the *Pastor of Hermas,* written undoubtedly by a Christian, seems to show clearly the influence of Qumran's doctrine of the Two Spirits working against each other in man, and the *Pastor's* conception of the Church as a body of penitents is almost a definition of the Community of the Alliance.[48] Literary contact with writings like the moral instructions of the *Manual* are entirely probable for the first century. It has even been suggested [49] that our gospel of St Matthew, 'a manual for teaching and administration within the Church', is a kind of *Manual of Discipline* for the Christian movement. It is certainly true that Matthew's use of the Old Testament, not as a source of rules for life, but as prophecy shown to be fulfilled, is not at all Rabbinic but entirely in keeping with the method of Qumran.

We cannot know how in fact Qumran and its sympathizers answered to the impact of Christ. We can

---

[48] On the literary relationship of the *Duae Viae* and of the *Pastor* to the *Manual of Discipline* cf. Audet, *Revue Biblique,* 1952, pp. 219-38; 1953, pp. 41-82.

[49] K. Stendahl, *The School of St. Matthew,* 1954.

only say that the spiritual fervour of the monks, their fraternal love, their pursuit of the heart's purity, their conviction of the power of God's grace (unstressed by the Pharisees), all these qualities made of them ideal soil for the seed of Christianity. They were truly God's poor, the poor who are pronounced blessed in the Beatitudes. Apt soil, one would have said, for the seed of the Word.

We do less than justice to the influence of the 'intertestamental' period if we are in fear of compromising the 'originality' of Christ—a convenient but dangerously vague term to which we shall have to return. But why draw the line at the Old Testament? Even if we are thinking in terms of time, which we are not, it might be well to remember that the two books of Maccabees belong to Qumran's period. If we are thinking, as we are, in terms of the Spirit's activity, we should avoid setting arbitrary limits: the gift of the Spirit is not confined to *Scriptural* inspiration. If Caiphas could speak 'not of himself' (John 11:51) but with the deep unheeded meaning of the Spirit, what of the most pious in Israel—of Essenism, of Qumran? The Word-made-flesh is not the beginning of revelation (it was the Word that was in the beginning) but its climax. We say all this not to settle a matter of fact (this must be done by a dispassionate comparison of Qumran and New Testament texts) but to declare a point of principle. Let us *suppose,* for instance, that Qumran associates the idea of suffering, even of the Isaian Suffering Servant, with the Messianic hope: what would this be but a great and truly biblical advance beyond the popular Davidic conception? And would the Spirit have nothing to do with it? And if our Lord were to have taken over the Qumran ideal, though with Jeremias and Job and Second Isaias before him he could never need to, and approved and lived it, we should not be surprised.

Let us have clearly in our minds what we mean by the 'originality' of Christ. Theologically speaking, our Lord was of course not only original but unique in his person and in his efficacious redemptive work. But what of his verifiable preaching? Now of our Lord's aphorisms it has been said that no single one of them cannot be paralleled, and often verbally paralleled, in rabbinic literature—and it would be rash to allege rabbinic dependence on Jesus. The originality lies not in these moral maxims but in all that lies behind them. Christ was not crucified for being a rabbi of the rabbis but for some bolder claim. It is not enough to say that Jesus and the Qumran sectaries have this in common: the sense of impending climax. The whole of the New Testament, not one passage here or there, drives home the central truth that Jesus himself *is* the climax. It is his exorcisms that show that the Kingdom has come, it is he who sees Lucifer falling from heaven, the Law and the Prophets were until John but with Jesus it is the time of the kingdom. It is this confident awareness of himself that lies behind all his moral demands with their authority and urgency and behind the assured conviction that his offer is unprecedented and unrepeatable: who does not gather with him scatters. In other words, 'the Christology lies behind the aphorisms, not ahead of them; this means that at no point is the literary or historical critic able to detect, in any stratum of the synoptic material, evidence that a Christological interpretation has been imposed upon an un-Christological history'.[50] If the teaching of Christ may be matched elsewhere in part and in detail it remains, in its ensemble and with the unique Christology that inspires and sustains it, an unrivalled body of teaching which is an objective and verifiable fact. In this it is 'original'. With it not even the whole rabbinic corpus has anything to compare—and certainly not the 'deep devotion, high hopes and pathetic aberrations' of Qumran. This is the true perspective which may have been, may still be, distorted in the present excitement. Within that perspective we may read with less disappointment

[50] Hoskyns and Davey, *The Riddle of the New Testament*, 1931, p. 145.

the rather negative conclusion of Burrows: 'Perhaps the best thing the Dead Sea Scrolls can do for us is to make us appreciate our Bible all the more by contrast.'

Now all this—the matter and manner of Christ's teaching in itself and as compared with that of others, of Qumran, for example—is the concern of the critical historian. He is not, however, professionally interested in the ultimate truth or falsehood of that teaching. In so far as this last is impervious to human reasoning it is the business of the historical philosopher: it is for him to contemplate the ruins and oblivion of Qumran and to contrast these with the enduring phenomenon of dynamic Christianity (which, in its turn, is only partially appreciable by the historical philosopher as such). He will then pronounce judgment upon the original worth of the two compared institutions, the dead and the living. This judgment will be still more valuable (other things being equal) if our philosopher has personally felt the dynamism of Christianity, for then he better understands one of the terms of his comparison.[51] Acceptance of this judgment is not, needless to say, an act of theological faith but an acquiescence of human reason. Nevertheless, it prepares for that faith—which, we must never forget, is a supernatural gift of God—and demonstrates that the act, when made, is not blind but a prudent human act made in accordance with right reason. By the act of theological faith itself we believe that Christ's truth is not merely superior to all that is most precious in Qumran but is itself an ultimate and an absolute. It is the Word itself.

---

[51] This against the allegation, which has been made once or twice, that those 'with religious commitments' are dangerous guides in this Qumran affair.

CHAPTER 10

The Word Made Flesh

THE Word that became incarnate in the flesh was
the Word that had spoken through Creation,
Law, Prophets. At that moment of incarnation it is
not surprising that the stage is lit by the two lamps
of Old Testament and New, the light of one soften-
ing or dissolving the shadows of the other. We could
choose no better scene to illustrate what has been
said of the Word that is never still, for ever adven-
turing, seeking new expressions and therefore new
creations, always teaching as it goes, leaving behind
it hints that have to be recovered and scrutinized
again. For this is the climax to which the Word was
working. The same Word that long ago had preached
the divine abandonment that brings life from poverty, suffering, death, now takes visible form to
practise it. In him must be embodied all that the
ancient Word commended, all that its hearers fell
short of. Without this, he is not the same Word.
And because he is the Word, he cannot return to
God void but, ascending on high again, must take
men captive with him. The Word that had been
descending in its parabola from the first moment of
creation, now in the moment we are considering it
touches the earth, afterwards it will curve upwards—
through how many years we do not know—bearing
what it has won, is winning, will win. A body of our
ancient stock is now established in a Paradise more
enduring than Adam's; such a body as God once
promised: You are dust and shall return to dust, is
now bidden: Sit at my right hand—and those in
Christ with him. But before this happy consumma-
tion there was much to be joyfully and painfully
done, and we shall now give our attention to the beginning of it all, to the instant when the Word once

commanded to 'dwell in Israel' makes his home in Mary in whom Israel comes to a point.

The formula of Duns Scotus is said to be the golden rule for Mary doctrine: 'It would seem justifiable to predicate the highest of Mary, provided this does not conflict with the authority of Church or of Scripture.' In this place, however, we are seeking not what the Scriptures allow us to say but what the Scriptures teach us to say. It is prudent to make this remark at the outset in order to remove the impression, or refute the charge, of minimizing where a mean view is most repugnant to the Catholic heart and mind. To consider Mary in the Scriptures is to contemplate the bud and not the bloom, though in the end we may find how surprisingly soon the bud started to open, because in the garden of Christian theology the Mary doctrine is a singularly precocious flower.

I have used the word 'theology' to kill with one blow the inarticulate, and proportionately dangerous, monster with the blasphemous name: 'Scripture and, after that, Theology.' The monster is real enough, as we all know. No, 'Mary in the Scripture' means 'Mary in official early Christian theology.' It follows, then, that we are not looking for bare facts but for theological interpretation of facts, an interpretation to which faith makes its response, which indeed compels faith, for the interpretation is official.

In what has just been said you will have noticed what seems to be a dishonest, and certainly convenient, fallacy. What, you may ask, has become of the Old Testament? Now it must be admitted that the exegete is often embarrassed by what appears to him a mistake of method in connection with the Mary doctrine. He feels strongly that it would be odd indeed if the Old Testament which only obscurely hints at a Word made flesh were to speak most clearly of the mother of the Word. The Old Testament, he says, is too often so used as to make it appear not only as anticipating the New, which is bad, but as excelling it, which is worse. Doubtless we are deal-

ing with a revelation that can break into any human
series, but Biblical experience teaches that even this
free revelation is adapted to its time, and without
overwhelming evidence we can make no exception
for one doctrine out of all the rest.

This is far from saying that the Old Testament
must not be used, only that it must not be used in
isolation. It has been said earlier that the Bible is
no juxtaposition of solid blocks of revelation, without life, without growth, without articulation. The
great stream of revelation cannot be frozen at some
given place and one slab of ice cut out of it that we
can call the Word of God. For in fact the Word is
not a word but a long sentence whose meaning is not
grasped until it is finished. This remains true whatever side we may take in the great *sensus plenior* or
'fuller sense', controversy which, some think, is little
more than a fight in the field of apologetics. In any
strong, conscious, literary tradition, *Z* in the series
may use *A* for his purposes, and thus force us back
to *A* to understand his terms. *A* himself must not be
used as an independent element unless we are clear
in our own minds that we are not going to read back
into him what we have already learned from *Z*.
Nevertheless, only *Z* plus *A* will yield us the meaning of *Z*. If this is true, in general, it is most certainly true of the Bible for which it has been abundantly demonstrated that the sacred authors are not
independent of their predecessors. If this is the case
with the Old Testament, how much more with the
New whose authors felt themselves the heirs of the
Old! The Christian Event dropped, as it were, into
the solution of the Old Testament and precipitated
what we see—a cloud of reference. Or, if you like,
it changed the water into wine. And in this process
the mother of Jesus was there.

Here, then, we have the basis for what has been
called 'anthological' exegesis which is most sound in
principle. But we must never forget that our feet are
now on a slippery path and that we are walking in a
world of allusion and subtlety. Many have and still

do proceed too fast and too confidently and, when they fall, discredit the way they have taken. Others, by careful and minute comparison of texts, will establish a case which is most impressive in detail but which may leave the more cautious still hesitant. To determine when subtlety has gone too far is not easy, except for those rash enough to suppose that no subtlety is required. Appeal will sometimes have to be made to a kind of sixth Scriptural sense which may admit one allusion and refuse the next. One may be uneasy or content with a reference to the famous oracle of Gen 3:15 as the background of Simeon's association of Mary with her son in the rise and fall of many in Israel; the same oracle may seem far from the woman clothed with the sun of Apoc 12, or from the 'woman' at Cana and the 'woman' at the foot of the Cross who, like Eve, became the mother of all the living. Within the last few years all these questions have been eagerly and competently discussed, and from the welter of divergence on detail there has emerged a conviction that the very early association of Eve with Mary and of Mary with the Church has very deep roots in the Scriptures. If it is impossible here to enter into the argument, it is at least prudent to record its outcome, this highest common factor of agreement which it would be foolish to discount on the ground that the reasoning is too subtle, namely that there is an interpenetration of Biblical thought between the collective 'woman' of Gen 3 who is to wage war on the serpent, the individual woman who became mother of the Saviour and again the collective woman, the spouse of Christ, the Church. It is unnecessary to recall that such interpretation of individual and collectivity is quite typical of Biblical literature. And so, to take one small example, it is not improbable that in the fourth Gospel, so profoundly symbolic, Mary stands for the Church when she asks that the water for the 'purifying of the Jews' should be changed into the wine of Christian sacrament.

But important as the fourth Gospel is in any discussion of Mary, we are going to concentrate our attention upon what, after all, is 'the unique Event in the sphere of soteriology and eschatology, which virtually contains all that follow',[1] I mean the Infancy narrative of Luke and in particular the Annunciation to Mary which has been called 'the parent cell' of this whole narrative.[2] For it has been well said that Mary's 'yes' on Calvary simply maintains the 'Fiat' of the Annunciation by which she acquiesced in the Incarnation and all its consequences whatever they might be.

It is here, if anywhere, that the employment of the Old Testament of which we have spoken has been brought into play. Its ideas and expressions have provided the raw material; the elder has been made to serve the younger: the first has become the last. In a recent and excellent study of the first two chapters of Luke [3] considerable attention has been given to this process known as *midrash,* that is to say the scrutiny of ancient texts for the benefit of a new situation. It is well known that early in the post-Exilic period this organization of old materials for a theological or apologetic purpose was already an entrenched method.[4] At the root of it all is the conviction that the word of God is living and valid for all times and applicable to all situations. Those who used this method were not at all concerned—as we are too much concerned—to analyze the conscious meaning of the ancient sacred author from whom they borrowed. In a sense the words were his property no longer—they had gone forth to perch wherever God made the dry land appear. And the New Testament in its turn takes up this tradition: it is confident of a God-given event to which the old God-

[1] K. Rahner, *Recherches de Science Religieuse*, XLII, 1954 p. 492.

[2] P. Benoit, *Revue Biblique*, 1958, p. 428.

[3] R. Laurentin, *Structure et Théologie de Luc I-II*, Paris 1957.

[4] Cf. R. Bloch, *Dictionnaire de la Bible, Supplement*, art Midrash.

given words cannot but be applicable. Its purpose in making use of this device may be apologetic, as in Matthew's Infancy narrative, or possibly (a theology with a conciliatory purpose) to comfort the converted, as in the Epistle to the Hebrews, but there is no doubt that Luke's purpose is wholly theological, and it is this theology we wish to examine. Since this is our aim, we need not attempt to assess the quantity of cold fact behind Luke's narrative; the sacred author is interpreting a situation and our main business is to arrive at his mind. But it should be said in passing, that the literary form he had chosen is by no means that of pure fiction: *midrash* does not simply invent, it investigates; it assumes a datum and seeks its significance.[5] We are free to question whether Luke is giving Mary's *ipsissima verba* when he writes: May it be done to me as you have said, or, How can this be done because man I do not know? We are still more free to reduce the pictorial element in, for example, the angel's apparition— though indeed it is not Luke's fault if we have exaggerated it. But we are not free to assert that the sacred author has misread the situation; there is a formal teaching here in an inspired theological source.

It might be remarked also that from the purely theological point of view the date of the Lucan Infancy narrative is only of importance in tracing the development of revelation. After all, what comes last in our present gospel story, the Resurrection, was the first in the evangelist's concern and the stimulant of penetration into all that preceded it. Theological thinking and writing travelled in an opposite direction to the historical sequence, passing from Resurrection to Transfiguration to Baptism to Annunciation. It is not surprising if the interest in Mary's function is relatively late in the New Testament period and that the Infancy narratives are the product

[5] J. Coppens, *Ephemerides Theologicae Lovanienses*, 1957, p. 733, is uneasy about the term *midrash* in connection with Luke 1-2; he fears that it is too strong and may mislead.

of reflection. Indeed, what at first sight might seem to cut us off from the earliest historical evidence—though this is far from being the case [6]—becomes an immeasurable theological gain. For the product of inspired reflection is to be preferred to the detail of inspired chronicle and allows, I should say it demands, closer literary analysis and a more profound examination. In these circumstances we should be very slow to accuse an exegesis of being too subtle.

After this long, but not unnecessary, preamble we may at last come to Luke's Infancy narrative itself. It has long been noticed that we have here a picture in two panels: the Baptist and Jesus.[7] There are two annunciations by Gabriel, two births, two circumcisions, two impositions of name. Each story ends with very similar words: The child grew and was strengthened in spirit; Jesus advanced in wisdom and age and grace with God and man. But there is contrast, too. For Elizabeth, however great her own son is to be, Mary is 'mother of my Lord'. The contrast is most notably brought out in the fashion of the two births: Elizabeth conceives a son in her old age but Mary conceives virginally. It reaches its climax in the titles of the two children: Prophet of the Most High, Son of the Most High. In short, Luke's attention is focused on the one whom the Baptist in later years was to declare 'greater than I' and the evangelist establishes this perspective right from the beginning, and since it *is* the beginning, Mary is involved.

Mary's situation is not unlike that of Daniel who 'kept silent and sought to understand the vision' (Dan 8:27), and indeed it seems certain that Luke is inviting the reader to think of Daniel. It is only

[6] The argument for an ancient Hebrew source (e.g. P. Winter, *New Testament Studies*, 1954, pp. 111-21) is impressive, though not conclusive (cf. P. Benoit, *New Testament Studies*, 1957, pp. 169-94). That Mary herself was ultimately a source of Luke's information seems certain; cf. Luke 2:10, 51 and the private character of the Annunciation.

[7] E.g. M-J. Lagrange, *Revue Biblique*, 1914, pp. 199-202.

in Daniel that the angel Gabriel appears, nowhere else in the Old Testament, and these are Gabriel's words:

> Seventy weeks have been decreed
> for your race and for the Holy City. . . .
> to bring in everlasting justice,
> to accomplish vision and prophecy,
> to anoint the holy of holies (Dan 9:24)

Gabriel's reappearance in Luke is certainly significant; it suggests that the seventy weeks are up, that the time is fulfilled (Luke uses the word five times in these two chapters) [8] and the holy of holies must be anointed. It is Gabriel's business to announce this to Mary. Now the ambiguity of Daniel's 'holy of holies' is well known,[9] it can stand for the holy place or priest. Luke seems deliberately to prefer the personal reference when, instead of writing 'therefore the child shall be called Son of God,' he gives us the awkward sentence, 'therefore the child shall be holy, shall be called Son of God.' One might go further and find that the evangelist sees a point in the seventy weeks also,[10] for if we accept the conventional thirty days to a month, the six months of Elizabeth's pregnancy before the Visitation, plus our Lady's own nine months, plus the forty days that elapsed before climactic Presentation, we reach Daniel's figure of 490 days. But here, it may be, we are going too far; Luke himself speaks of five months in connection with Elizabeth (1:24) and it is *in the course* of the sixth that Mary visits her. We may therefore discountenance this ingenious calculation, but the substantial parallel still remains. To Daniel who 'kept these things in his heart' (Dan 7:28) Gabriel appeared to declare the fullness of time; to Mary who 'kept all these things in her heart' (Luke 2:51)

---

[8] Luke 1:23, 57; 2:6, 21, 22.

[9] Cf. *Bible de Jérusalem*, note *ad. loc.*

[10] E. Burrows, S.J., *The Gospel of the Infancy*, London, 1940, pp. 41-2. Laurentin, *op. cit.*, favours the view.

Gabriel appeared to announce that the time was fulfilled. For the first revelation God chose a man after
his own heart (cf. Dan 9:23), for the second he
chose a maiden, an obedient handmaid of the Lord.

But it is a commonplace that the first two chapters
of Luke are a tissue of Biblical reminiscence. If
anyone doubts it he may glance down the margins
of the *Bible de Jérusalem* where he will find seventy
Old Testament references, and the list is not exhaustive. Now if this is true of the peripheral material, it
should be at least equally true of the heart, which is
Gabriel's annunciation to Mary. And in fact at least
three texts compete for the privilege of being Luke's
source [11]; of these the two short triumphant messianic psalms with which the oracles of Sophonias
ended [12] come nearest to the angel's message:

Cry out for joy, daughter of Sion,
Shout for gladness, O Israel.
Rejoice . . . O daughter of Jerusalem,
Yahweh is king of Israel in your midst (lit: in
your womb)

On that day they shall say to Jerusalem:
Fear not, O Sion. . . .
Yahweh your God is in your midst (lit: in your
womb),
a mighty Saviour (Heb: *Yoshia'*)

Before we quote Luke's text we must recall a point
made by Père Lyonnet twenty years ago [13] in respect
of the translation: *Ave* Maria, *Hail* Mary. For Luke's

[11] Soph 3:14-17; Joel 2:21-7; Zach 9:9-10. A schematic
'synopsis of contacts' is to be found in Laurentin, *op. cit.*, p. 66,
footnote 8.

[12] The present ending of Sophonias seems to reflect the Exilic
period (Soph 3:18b-20).

[13] S. Lyonnet, *Chaire Kecharitomene*, Biblica, XX, 1939, pp.
131ff. The point is taken up by Laurentin. Audet, in *Revue
Biblique*, 1956, p. 357, evidently regrets Osty's Salut!' in the
Bible de Jérusalem translation of Luke 1:28.

chaire is not a polite introduction, a 'good-morning', translating the Hebrew *shalom*. This last is customarily rendered *eirene,* Peace! What we have just translated 'Cry out for joy' is, in the Septuagint, *chaire sphodra.* The word *chaire,* therefore, has a strong sense, it is an invitation to rejoice in the prospect of messianic times. We may now consider Gabriel's message:

> Rejoice, *kecharitomene,*
> The Lord (Yahweh) is with you. . . .
> Fear not, O Mary. . . .
> You shall conceive in your womb
> and bear a son.
> And you shall give him the name:
> Yahweh the Saviour (Heb: *yeshua'*)

To confirm the likeness to the Sophonias text, it has been rightly pointed out that with Zachary Gabriel is content with 'your wife shall bear you a son', whereas with Mary he uses a tautology, uncharacteristic of Luke, that has its best explanation in the reference back to Sophonias which, in any case, it is hard to refuse.

To what purpose is Luke's deliberate assumption of the Old Testament text? Clearly, of course, to signal the advent of messianic times. But may we draw any further conclusions? Does Luke want us to consider Mary more closely? If this question means: Does Luke want us to contemplate Mary in isolation and for her own sake? the answer is plainly 'No'. It would distort the whole perspective of the *euaggelion.* We cannot judge Elizabeth or Simeon or Anna except in relation to the Child; we cannot judge Mary either. Nevertheless, as this relationship is less or more intimate, the focus and magnification of the related figure is sharper and greater as it comes nearer to the Child. Now it is surely not incautious to suppose that Luke is thinking of Mary as the daughter of Sion of whom Sophonias is speaking: Rejoice, daughter of Sion; Rejoice, *kecharitomene*;

Fear not, O Sion; Fear not, O Mary. Sion, your God
is in your womb, a mighty saviour; You shall conceive in your womb and bear a son and call him
Yahweh the saviour. Mary is the locus of God's salvation, the place from which his active Word was to
go: *The Law will go forth from Sion, and the word
of Yahweh from Jerusalem.* But the prophetic passage we have quoted is introduced by an oracle on
the Remnant of Israel, the residue that survives, ever
diminishing, after a series of trials at the hand of
history, a remnant in which (as the progressive revelation of the Old Testament instructs us) membership
is achieved by humility and complete submission to
God:

> In your midst I shall leave
> only a people that is humble and lowly,
> looking to Yahweh for its protection,
> the remnant of Israel. (Soph 3:12)

Following this reductive tendency of the Old Testament doctrine, the New finds its ultimate goal in one
who is the ideal Remnant:

> The promises were addressed to Abraham
> and to his seed.
> Scripture does not say 'to his seeds',
> as if thinking of several,
> but indicates only one: 'to his seed',
> that is to say, Christ (Gal 3:16)

Had Luke been asked to identify the Remnant he
would surely have pointed to all the humble figures
of his Infancy narrative who, he makes it clear, were
eagerly awaiting the consolation of Israel: Zachary,
Elizabeth, Simeon, Anna—and of these Mary with
her canticle of humility is evidently, for Luke, at
once the humblest and the greatest. He would not
disagree with Paul: the summit of the pyramid is
Christ but the single stone beneath the summit is
Mary. The daughter of Sion on the threshold of the
latter days brings forth only one child; the daughter

is no longer many but one. Given this descent from the collective to the individual within a literary tradition in which the collectivity and the individual tend to fuse, it may be after all, though one has long doubted it, that 'the woman clothed with the sun' of Apoc 12 is a truly polyvalent symbol in the Johannine manner, referring simultaneously, in the literal sense, to the Old and New Israel with its crown of twelve tribes and twelve apostles, and also to Mary, the ideal Sion, mother of one who gave power to all who believed in him to become sons of God.[14]

If such is indeed Luke's mind, the way is open— though it will need to be trod carefully—to a collective interpretation of other texts in which Mary appears. In the Magnificat, for example, Mary's 'my spirit rejoices in God my Saviour' will suggest Israel's canticle in Heb 3:18: 'I will be glad in the Lord, rejoice in God my Saviour'; 'he has looked upon the lowliness of his handmaid' will recall: 'Yahweh has looked upon our lowliness and brought us out of Egypt' (Deut 26:7): and the 'handmaid of the Lord' will find its counterpart in Israel's proudest title, the *ebed Yahweh,* the servant of the Lord, which Mary herself uses (Luke 1:54) when in her canticle she passes so naturally, but to us oddly, from herself to all Israel. It may even be that Simeon's 'a sword shall pass through your soul' is meant to echo the sentence of Ezechiel (14:17): 'a sword shall pass through the land (of Israel).[15] It is true that the further we advance in this process the more extravagant it seems to become, but the practice of pirouettes may teach us to walk gracefully, and to write poetry may perfect our prose; if we explore all the possibilities of a text it will at least help us to appreciate the probabilities and identify the certainties.

Among the probabilities one is tempted to rank a

[14] Cf. L. Cerfaux, *La Vierge dans l'Apocalypse*, Ephemerides Theologicae Lovanienses, 1955, pp. 21-23.

[15] Cf. Laurentin, *op. cit.*, pp. 89-90.

profound and technical sense attributed to Gabriel's *episkiasei:* the power of the Most High will *over-shadow* you.[16] It is suggested that the daughter of Sion is thus characterized not as mother, though the ideas are not unconnected, but as the home of a great presence. The word is unusual (four times in the Greek Old Testament) and appears to have its most technical meaning in Exod 40:34 f:

Then the cloud covered the Tent of Assembly
and the glory of Yahweh filled the Dwelling,
And Moses could not enter the Tent of Assembly,
because of the cloud that *overshadowed* it
and of the glory of Yahweh with which the Dwell-
    ing was filled.

This 'cloud' sign of the divine presence is a frequent Old Testament symbol; we meet it again on the mount of Transfiguration, and a voice speaks from it: This is my beloved son. If we accept this Exodus reference in Luke's words, there is no doubt that Mary is presented to us as the shrine of the divine presence, the ark of God's covenant. Perhaps we may go further, though here with much more cau- tion. The story of David's reception of the Ark (2 Sam 6:2-11) may lie behind Luke's account of the Visitation, as Fr Burrows suggested twenty years ago.[17] If we accept this, David's 'How is it that the Ark of Yahweh should come to me?' is deliberately echoed by Elizabeth's 'How is it that the mother of my Lord should come to me?'; David's 'skipping' (unusual word) before the ark is matched by the Baptist's 'skipping' at the sound of Mary's voice, and the ark's three-month stay with Obed-Edom is paral- leled by Mary's three months with Elizabeth. *Qui potest capere, capiat.*

We have shown with more or less probability and

16 Cf. Laurentin, *op. cit.,* pp. 73-9. Lyonnet, *Le récit de l'An-nonciation,* L'Ami du Clergé, 1956, pp. 43-4. E. Burrows, *op. cit.,* pp. 107ff.

17 Burrows, *op. cit.,* pp. 47ff.

more or less conviction how the Old Testament text
has been summoned to the help of the New. We
may now ask if there is any Old Testament *literary
form* that can come to our assistance; has Luke been
guided by the Old Testament in this field also? We
cannot forego the question even if we refuse the answer, for the identification of literary form is the first
business of the interpreter, it is the outer key to the
author's mind. The question has been most competently discussed in a recent article, the value of which
is not diminished by a conclusion which may seem
to many, and to myself I confess, extravagant.[18] The
author distinguishes the three literary forms of
dream, message, prophecy, and points out that in all
three the initiative is God's, that the message, unlike
the dream, involves dialogue since it is delivered in
waking hours, that again unlike the dream the message is considered clear as soon as the messenger departs. The parallel chosen for the message to Mary
is taken from the annunciation to Gideon in Jg 6:
11-24, which we abbreviate here:

> Gideon was threshing wheat in the winepress
> to hide it from the Midianites. And the angel of
> Yahweh appeared to him and said: 'Yahweh is
>   with you,
> valiant hero!' 'With all respect, my Lord,'
>   answered
> Gideon, 'If Yahweh is with us, how is it that all
>   this
> is happening to us?' . . . . And the angel of
>   Yahweh said
> to him: 'Go . . . and save Israel from the hand of
>   Midian.'
> 'How am I to save Israel . . . I am the least in
>   my father's
> house,' said Gideon, 'If I have found favour in
>   your
> eyes, give me a sign that it is you who speak.'

[18] J. P. Audet, 'L'Annonce à Marie', *Revue Biblique*, 1956,
pp. 346-74.

It will be noticed that the angel's 'Yahweh is with you' is not a mere greeting nor even a compliment but a promise—or rather, for the point to me does not seem unimportant—a declaration of present fact with future consequences. It will be observed, too, that Gideon is not addressed by his own name; he is given a name, 'Valiant Hero', that evidently does not recall his past history but indicates the part he is now to assume. Gideon then asks, 'How can this be?' and a sign is given him. Mary's situation is strangely like. Gideon is chosen for *a* messianic deliverance, Mary is chosen for *the* messianic deliverance (Luke 1:31-3). The first word of the angel's message is in each case a presage of this liberation, for there is little doubt that the word we translate 'Hail' sounds the messianic note (cf. *supra*). Nor does Gabriel use Mary's name at the outset, as he did not use Gideon's; instead, he greets her with a name of portent: it was 'Valiant Hero' before, it is *Kecharitomene* now. Mary asks 'How can this be?' and a sign, though unasked (and in this she shows more than Gideon's simplicity), is given her.

The first and most general conclusion one might draw from this parallel is by no means the least important, and here is the place for a remark to be made which we have already made more than once. Behind the earliest sources of our Christian doctrine, and therefore behind our Mary doctrine, there lies the Semitic mind which does not address itself to the definition of being but to the significance of action. We shall have to be careful, therefore, when we use the Greek word 'theology' that we strip it of all its speculative relationships. Our biblical theology is not speculative but functional. The difference may be simply illustrated by contrasting the expressions, 'the second person of the Trinity' and 'the Word of God'; the first is an attempt at definition, the second describes a function; the first is Greek, the second Semitic. Now if this is true of the central figure of Biblical revelation, it will be most certainly true of all the others. We shall not expect, then, to find in

our early sources an *analysis* of Mary's dignity—
much less a treatise on her personal sanctity—but a
statement of her function and a description of her
action. Now in the Annunciation narrative we are,
if I may put it so, at two removes from the Mary
doctrine as we know it today. There is this first remove we have just spoken of, and there is a second
remove that is the result of the literary form of messianic annunciation. For in this second, it is not the
personality of the messianic instrument that occupies
the true centre but, in Gideon's case, the liberating
action of God, in Mary's the child who is to occupy
once for all the throne of David—and as such may
be called 'Son of the Most High' (Luke 1:32-3)—
and who, furthermore, is to be 'son of God' in a quite
transcendental sense (Luke 1:35). It is, I hope,
needless to say that one is not questioning our Lady's
creaturely unrivalled holiness. For despite all the
reserves we have made, it still remains clear even to
the casual reader of Luke that Mary's own person
has for him a special interest and stands out uniquely from its distinguished entourage: Elizabeth, Simeon, Anna; and Luke could not have given her
greater praise than to put the *Magnificat* into her
mouth. But when we are speaking of Mary in the
Scriptures, the Scriptural emphasis must be preserved.

These remarks have a particular application also.
They have to do with a word we have so far refused
to translate: the word *kecharitomene*. Père Audet,
in the article I have mentioned, here gives us a timely
warning. He deprecates a sentence like this, for example: 'The grace of which the Virgin is "full" is
that which Paul speaks of in Eph 1:6, the grace that
makes us pleasing in the eyes of God. . . . *kecharitomene* indicates a permanent state of possession of
grace not in the physical but in the moral order.'
And indeed this does seem to be approaching the
word from the wrong end, as it were; it is as if we
were to understand 'Peace to men of good-will' making the 'good-will' man's and not God's. In fact,

kecharitomene (if we are to judge by the parallel
with Gideon and from the situation as a whole) is a
title conferred, a portentous name as Abraham's and
Israel's and Peter's were, a name expressing a function allotted by God, not a compliment to Mary for
the way she had qualified for that function. The
messianic 'Rejoice' is immediately followed by this
word, and conveys to it its own messianic flavour;
in two words Mary has the substance of the angel's
message: there is to be a messianic deliverance and
she is chosen for its instrument, she is *kecharitomene*,
privileged; God's choice has fallen upon her. What
came before this choice, what prompted it, Luke
leaves us to conjecture only. It is true that such
submission as Mary's is not the work of one day but
of years. As for what came after the choice, the
fourth Gospel will lift the curtain twice: the mother
of the One was to become the mother of the many-
in-the-One. But here in the Annunciation narrative
Luke places the Messiah himself in the centre of the
stage. Undoubtedly Mary is for him the queen-
mother, the *gebirah,* or Great Lady, of Judah's
court,[19] but his light is turned directly upon the King,
whose mother it is Mary's highest privilege to be.
Luke makes us aware of her, there on her throne in
the fringe of the light, but she does not distract us—
she never could—from her royal son.

When we move from Luke's theological field on to
the ground of chronicle we are much less at our ease.
Once it has been established that we have to do with
midrash, the quantity of 'cold fact' becomes a problem, though of relatively small importance as some
would hold. It is many years now since Ladeuze
very cautiously suggested that the *Magnificat* may
not have been spoken by Mary at the time, but

[19] Cf. Elizabeth's 'Mother of my Lord', i.e. of my lord the
king; Cerfaux, *Recueil Lucian Cerfaux* (Gembloux 1954), I, 50.
For the *gebirah* cf. R. de Vaux, *Les Institutions de l' Ancien
Testament* (Paris 1958), pp. 180-2. In Solomon's reign Bath-
sheba was *gebirah,* and Solomon had her sit at his right hand
(I [III] Kings 2:19).

towards the end of her life when she had meditated on all that had happened since her son's birth.[20] On the other hand, few scholars today would ascribe the canticle to Elizabeth and thus cripple the march of the narrative; nevertheless it is now considered a legitimately debatable question whether the *Magnificat* represents not Mary's *ipsissima verba* (as many of our Lord's own sayings are not) but an interpretation of her mind by Luke or by his source, or an adapted pre-existing Jewish hymn (Benoit) perhaps (P. Winter) of Maccabean origin. Or, to take another example, it may be argued that the famous 'How can this be done because man I do not know?' is a hinge-verse of Luke's designed to lead the reader from the Jewish messianism of the first half of Gabriel's message to the second half with its transcendental messianism. Those who hold that all these questions are secondary point out that the object of our search is the theology of the New Testament and not the chronicle of detail, an inspired interpretation of the facts which is for us a norm of faith and a seed of faith's growth. This is true, though it would be prudent to recall that the interpretation presupposes certain facts that are to be interpreted. Among these facts the reader of Luke would be inclined to rank the state of Mary's mind not after the Resurrection but at the time of which we speak. Luke scrupulously observes it on more than one occasion when the reader may feel it is not particularly necessary for his theological purpose. 'As for Mary, she treasured up all these things and pondered them in her heart'; 'The child's father and mother stood amazed at the things that were being said about him'; 'But they did not understand what he had said to them'; 'His mother stored up all these things in her heart'.[21] It is therefore difficult to believe that in the Annunciation narrative Luke presents Mary merely as a passive figure, a pivot for the

[20] J. Coppens, *art. cit.*, p. 731.
[21] Luke 2:19, 33, 50, 51.

angelic message, and not as a creature of flesh and blood, intelligence and will.

It may therefore be considered a legitimate question to ask what Mary's own reaction was to Gabriel's words. Are we to gather that she understood, for example, the subtle Old Testament allusion to the *shekinah,* or divine indwelling within her (a contested allusion even now, we must remember) and carried it to its full conclusion, the divinity of her son? Now the question is perhaps legitimate, as we have said, but is it well put? We have spoken of the functional nature of Semitic theology. Would Mary have asked, 'How shall I define the nature of this child'? Would she not ask rather (as she did), 'Where is he to come from?' and ask herself, 'What is he destined for?' The answer to the first came from Gabriel, to the second from Simeon also: 'You see this child? He is destined for the fall and for the rising of many in Israel, a sign that is denied.' It is true to say, to use our Greek terms, that the second person of the Blessed Trinity could have assumed an already constituted adult human nature, but if in fact (as Mary well knew) this new creature comes so uniquely from God, what is she to think of it but that it is like and unlike all others, uniquely related to God? A divine, privileged, private, unmentioned revelation is beyond the reach of the interpreter who has to be content to note that the mind of a young Jewish girl, even so near to God, could scarcely go further. And hers would be an intuitive and not a discursive theology—or rather she would learn by a series of intuitions which Luke hints at broadly enough, a series of which the Annunciation is first and greatest, intuitions sad and joyful, Cana, Cross, Resurrection, what it was to be the mother of such a child and what the child was whom she had mothered. Once again granted the legitimacy of the initial question, she could not possibly have misunderstood that she was to be mother of the Messiah, for the Messiah is defined by his function, but the perception of divinity in our formulated sense is quite another matter. Quite apart from the inconceivability of daily intercourse between a creature and one known to be God (for imagination is no fair argument), we have no strictly exegetical proof that Mary did not grow as the Apostles grew to know her son as God's word, God's unique expression of himself, God's son with the incommunicable name of Lord, only when the Resurrection had solved all riddles.

But what of the second half of Mary's mind? How did she understand herself, and by that I mean her function? This perception of hers is interpreted to us primarily in the great 'Fiat' of Luke 1:38 by which she establishes her position in the divine redemptive plan, a position theologians will discuss until the end of time and which the Church's own living will increasingly declare. But this is the great conclusion and climax to which the dialogue sweeps only after its momentary rest and hesitation that sets it on its way again: 'How can this be done, for man I do not know?' These four words, *epei andra ou ginosko,* have provoked volumes of discussion for which, it must be firmly stated, there is room. For if we may speak of 'tradition' in this matter, we must realize that we are speaking not of a dogmatic tradition but of an interpretational one which, moreover, cannot be traced back further than Ambrose. We are therefore driven back to the text. The theories range from 'interpolation' to 'vow'. Interpolation we need not consider: our business is to interpret the text as it stands which, moreover, is a powerfully forged unity. The 'vow' (or, more cautiously, the 'intention') of virginity theory is the view of many Catholic scholars with not a few notable exceptions.[22] Now it is not true that the opposition to the 'vow' hypothesis is based on a refusal to accept a private revelation made to Mary before the Annunciation,

[22] On various views cf. P. F. Ceuppens, *De Mariologia Biblica* (Turin & Rome 1951), pp. 68-74; U. Holzmeister, *Verbum Domini,* 1939, p. 74; M. Zerwick, Notes *ad usum privatum,* 1955. The last, pp. 123f., makes the objection referred to in the sentence following.

though it should be observed that an exegetical position is weakened by conjecture. The main difficulty is not of supposing a revelation but of accounting for the betrothal entered into before the Annunciation despite an existing vow of virginity made (unless we suppose an Annunciation before the Annunciation) quite blindly. In the hypothesis of a pious 'intention' of virginity with no private revelation required, the betrothal is still more strange. On the other hand, what is Mary's difficulty if she is betrothed and intends to marry in the ordinary way?

Père Audet's solution is surprising and one hesitates to accept it. We must, he says, re-translate *epei andra ou ginosko:* 'How can this be done, *for in that case I must not know man?*' The apparent artificiality of this use of *epei,* or at least the seeming overloading of the word, he justifies by appeal to the Pauline use.[23]

Why Mary should say such a thing must be explained, Père Audet continues, not from a reconstruction of the 'facts' by conjecture (though one may feel that we are dangerously near it) but by an inquiry into Luke's mind as betrayed by his use of narrative, identical in literary form, of the annunciation to Gideon (Jg 6:11-24). Gideon as he threshed, so unusually, not on the exposed hill-top open to any Midianite observer, had Israel's liberation very much on his mind; to this mentality the angel was the answer, for the literary form of annunciation, like that of prophecy and dream, presents God's rejoinder to man's thought. Gideon's objection is: 'I am the least in my father's house'; Mary's is *epei andra ou ginosko.* Mary belonged to that expectant group which Luke describes; she too was longing to see 'the Christ of the Lord', but she knew and had ruminated the prophecy of Is 7:14. At present she was no more than betrothed, she could be the *'almah* of Isaias, but she was betrothed with a view to mar-

---

[23] I Cor 5:10; 7:14 etc. To many the usage will seem too erudite within the literary style of the Infancy narrative.

riage—and this was evidently now excluded if she understood Gabriel and Isaias correctly. She therefore replies quite naturally, 'How can this be done, for in that case I must not know man?' (i.e., get married). Now if one disagrees with this view it is certainly not because an intention to marry on the part of Mary is unthinkable. We must not confuse Mary's mind before the Annunciation with her mind after it. That she was in fact always a virgin is a datum of our faith and perhaps has some textual support in our Lord's final committal of his mother not to a brother but to John. It may be that Luke represents her as perceiving the force of an angelic reference to a divine indwelling, a contact with the divine which excluded the close human relation we speak of.[24] But it is not necessary to assume all this. After all, the knowledge that God had chosen her for such a purpose would surely fill her with a sense of sacredness such as a woman would understand and a man like Joseph respect. But to declare the opinion impious which holds that Mary, as yet unaware of her high destiny, intended marriage would betray an outlook far from robust and reverent. No, one's hesitation when confronted with Audet's view is linguistic, together with some misgiving about Mary's (or Luke's) conjectured reflection on the *almah* oracle. Somewhere behind the *epei andra ou ginosko* must lie a Hebrew *chi lo yada'ti ish,* or *chi enenni yada'ath ish* which could scarcely bear the weight Luke is supposed to have put upon it. And so for Mary's meditation of Isaias, one feels that Luke will have left too much to the intelligence of his readers. Despite Lagrange's rejection[25] and Laurentin's casual dismissal of it,[26] the opinion of Cajetan, taken

---

[24] Abstention was prescribed by Moses before the cloud descended on Sinai (Ex 19:15f.; and cf. I Sam [Kings] 21:5; Lev 22:3).

[25] *Evangile selon Saint Luc*, note to Luke 1:34. The author concedes 'exegetical probability' to the view and underlines its orthodoxy, quoting St Ambrose.

[26] *Op. cit.,* p. 178.

up by Gunkel, seems the most natural one. If we may take Audet's own example from Gideon, it appears clear that the angel's word is immediately operative—as one might expect God's word to be; that very night Gideon gave the signal for revolt. We may assume the same for Mary; the delay, a literary delay after all, is negligible; we are surely meant to think, and she is surely presented as thinking, that the conception awaits only her Fiat. Gabriel's future tense, 'You shall conceive', is not more future than his 'You shall be dumb' addressed to Zachary and simultaneously effective; the sense of Mary's 'I know not man' is 'I am not in the married state'.

We hope that all that has been said has put Mary where she would want to be, that is to say in the heart of God's plan to save all men. If we have turned the light from her to what surrounds her and what is within her (as if this were possible), it is only to see how, in the Psalmist's words, *mirabilis est Deus in sanctis suis,* God is glorious in his sanctuary. We have only stolen Mary's own way: the Lord has looked upon the worthlessness of his handmaid. Even Christ, in the end, will present his kingdom to the Father, and God will be all in all (I Cor 15:28).

I should like to quote a Biblical scholar who is not a Catholic:

> She is the one who bears Christ within her; but she has no desire to keep him for herself for she is, after all, the one who gives him to the world. In this way she, like the Church, plays her part in what may be called God's 'conspiracy' to save the world, and she may be honoured as the woman who, in all secrecy, set Christ among men, Christ in whom the kingdom of God is present. What the Church will be until Christ's return, she has already been: the smuggler of heaven.[27]

[27] J.-J. von Allmen, *Vocabulaire Biblique,* p. 198.

It is strange how one can never think or write of Mary without being forced back to an inspection of foundations — apologetical, exegetical, theological. There is something provocative about her. She provokes whole volumes on the development of dogma,[28] re-examinations of the Redemption doctrine, questions of interpretational procedure (as we have just seen). But above all she is that historical person who is the terminus—and the beginning—of God's climactic 'interference' in human history. She stands stubbornly, a virgin with child, asserting that 'interference' in herself. There is a demythicization which is in principle legitimate and certainly fashionable. The Church has not defined the limits to which it may go, but Mary is there as the fortified place past which it must not. She remains the guardian of the historical Christ, the witness and custodian and minister of the Word.

[28] E.g. C. Dillenschneider, *Le Sens de la Foi et le Progrès Dogmatique du Mystère Marial*, Rome, 1954.

CHAPTER 11

The Word in the Church

TO many Christians there is nothing more provocative than the Catholic doctrine of Mary. Amongst the more thoughtful the opposition is maintained in good faith. But it is surely not that those who love Christ despise his mother: after all, the perpetual virginity of Mary was stoutly sustained by the earliest Reformers, and there is the gospel of John to defend her influence with her son. No, there is some profound difference of principle here, and we must try to identify it. If there is a quarrel, let us find out what it is all about; some quarrels, and this is one of them, are symptoms of deeper antagonism. Moreover, if we pursue the quest for the origins of this profound difference, we may find our own mind too—a discovery of some importance. And lest emotion sway judgment or embitter argument, we must try for the moment to forget how deeply we Catholics are wounded by this attitude and how the world is impoverished by a grudging approach to Mary. Instead, we shall take the Mary doctrine tranquilly as a starting-point: first to show negatively how the Catholic does not flout the Word of God; secondly to explain the positive Catholic approach to the interpretation of the Word. We ask not necessarily for agreement but for sympathetic understanding.

Some time ago, British Television presented a play called 'Family Portrait'. It assumed that our Lady had other children than Jesus. Naturally there were protests, particularly from Catholic correspondents. But it would be harsh to blame the playwright. Even the most conscientious of dramatists would take his lead from the authorities of his own persuasion. In Cadoux's Pelican *Life of Jesus* he would read:

With some hesitation I incline to the belief that Mary was Joseph's only wife and that Jesus and all his brothers and sisters were her children.

In Vincent Taylor's scholarly commentary on St Mark's gospel he would find much the same:

There can be little doubt that the Helvidian view (i.e., that Mary had other children) stands as the simplest and most natural explanation of the references to the brothers of Jesus in the Gospels.[1]

And it would be not rash to say that this represents a view common among Christian Scripture scholars.

The letters of Catholic objectors quite justly called attention to the word *adelphos*. They repeatedly and correctly pointed out that the translation 'brother', though generously maintained in the Catholic versions, is of doubtful accuracy.[2] The argument was based not so much on the Greek—which has its own word for 'cousin'—as on the Semitic word, Hebrew or Aramaic, that lies behind the Greek.[3] The appeal is not unreasonable. The first use of the term in the gospels in connection with our Lord is found in Mark 3:31, and Taylor says of this passage: 'Long before Mark incorporated it in his gospel the narrative was current and gained its form in oral tradition.' We are pointed back therefore if not to the Aramaic language itself at least to an Aramaic background. Hesitation is therefore justified. Nor is the Catholic alone in his caution. In a recent Swiss

---

[1] Cf. C. J. Cadoux, *The Life of Jesus* (Penguin, 1958), p. 34; and V. Taylor, *The Gospel according to St. Mark* (London, 1953), p. 249.

[2] But who can measure its impact on even the most detached scholars?

[3] There is no need to add to the instances so often cited of the use of *'ah* (Hebrew), and *'aha* (Aramaic) or — in the Septuagint — of *adelphos*; cf. examples in M.-J. Lagrange, *L'Evangile selon S. Marc*, 1929, p. 80.

Protestant publication a contributor, who is also the editor, writes:

> With the problem of deciding whether or not Mary had other children the New Testament is not concerned . . . It does not hesitate to speak of the brothers and sisters of the Lord but without specifying whether they were children of Joseph by a previous marriage or whether they were cousins— an opinion which is exegetically defensible by reason of the elasticity of relationship terms in the Jewish world.[4]

On this point discussion has reached saturation, but perhaps we may be allowed to recall two passages of *Mark* which can scarcely be absolved from the debate. The villagers of Nazareth are reported: 'Is not this the carpenter, the son of Mary and brother of James and Joses?' (6:3). And, in the same Gospel, those standing by the Cross include 'Mary the mother of James and Joses' (15:40). Of this second passage Taylor remarks: 'Mark would not have designated Mary the Virgin in this roundabout manner.' He is therefore obliged, since he has adopted the Helvidian view, to distinguish the pair of brothers in chapter 6 from the pair in chapter 15. The distinction is of course possible but we may be excused for sensing a *tour de force*.

But here is a warning that may be timely: the charge that Scripture disproves the perpetual virginity of Mary was so heartily answered that readers of the correspondence may have been led to think that Scripture, I mean Scripture as a lonely letter, was held to prove it positively. Now this, as we hope to show, is no necessary part of the Catholic claim, a fact that should be made clear for the sake not less of others than of ourselves. It is true that if our Lady's 'I know not man' (Luke 1:34) implies a vow

---

[4] J. J. con Allmen, *Vocabulaire Biblique*, Neuchatel, 1954, p. 197.

of virginity, we have the beginning of a positive argument from explicit Scripture—but to demonstrate this implication seems difficult to some, and to many others, impossible.[5] Be that as it may, we should do well to remember that the argument from the wide possibility of the term *adelphos* is a negative one only. In any case, that blood-brothers are not mentioned does not prove they did not exist, and even if they did not exist (may it be said with reverence) we have still to prove perpetual virginity. It is vital to the Catholic position that Scripture should not contradict dogma; it is not part of that position to maintain that the private exegete, left to his own interpretative resources, can deduce from Scripture the dogma's positive demonstration. Hence, as Lagrange noted many years ago: 'Theologians do not exaggerate the significance of the Scriptural *data* because, as they uniformly recognize, the perpetual virginity of Mary is a dogma based rather on Tradition than on Scripture.'[6]

It would prolong or frustrate this essay to enter into the evidence from early tradition. It is enough to note in passing that Hegesippus, writing between 174 and 189 A.D., makes it sufficiently clear that James—who, if any, was blood-brother of the Lord —was in fact the Lord's cousin; that Clement of Alexandria was asserting in 200 A.D. that James was son of Joseph and not of Mary; that Origen who, in 203 succeeded Clement as headmaster in Alexandria, wrote with regard to Mark 3:31: 'I consider it is fitting that Jesus should have among men the first fruits of chaste purity that Mary had among women.' One recalls these testimonies with a very modest purpose: merely to warn the opponents of Mary's virginity that the mention of a few names will not suffice ('Tertullian, Helvidius, Bonosus and Jovinianus and others'; Taylor, p. 248). Tertullian (c. 220 A.D.) had

---

[5] Cf. the preceding chapter.
[6] M.-J. Lagrange, *L'Evangile selon S. Marc.* p. 86.

an axe to grind and was no 'man of the Church' as Jerome pointed out; Helvidius does not speak until one hundred and sixty years later. The serious scholar will certainly not be impressed by the two names from the end of the fourth century: Bonosus, the rather obscure heretic and later schismatic, was condemned for this very opinion by his contemporaries; Jovinianus, an ex-monk of wild immoral habits cut a poor figure in a gallery of witnesses. 'And others' is rather too anonymous for discussion. But we repeat that we are content to defend on this ground where we could reasonably mount an attack. Indeed we might have forgone even the defence were not Cadoux's *Life of Jesus* in so many hands:

> The catholic idea is (he writes) that because Mary was the Saviour's mother it would have been unseemly for Joseph to have had intercourse with her after Jesus' birth or for her to have borne more children. . . . This is but another example of making doctrinal fitness do duty for historical evidence and it is of no authority whatever. It is not suggested by anything in Scripture.[7]

What does the author mean when he speaks of 'doctrinal fitness doing duty for historical evidence'? After all, we have seen some of the historical evidence and—for what historical evidence is worth in a case of this kind—it is more impressive for the doctrine than the corresponding evidence against it. As for 'doctrinal fitness', it is true that Origen has adduced this very reason—among others—but could his ideal, however appealing, have stood against the known facts and against clearly decisive texts from the Scriptures? Or is it not possible that the facts as known to him in 203 A.D. bade him seek the fitness

---

[7] C. J. Cadoux, *op. cit.*, p. 34. 'Suggested in Scripture' is not in any case satisfactory evidence for Cadoux. The virginal conception of our Lord is more than 'suggested' but the author denies it on the ground that the Lucan story 'bristles with historical improbabilities'

of the facts? In any case, let us at least insist that
this despised 'doctrinal fitness' argument be barred
not to one side only but to both. We, for our part,
have equal right to refuse the proffered argument of
Taylor: 'The fact that Jesus had blood brothers and
sisters, it may be held, underlines the reality and
completeness of the Incarnation.' But, to be plain,
this argument does not attain the stature even of
'doctrinal fitness'. Do we need subsequent births to
prove that a first was 'real and complete'?

Catholics have said all these things a thousand
times and still the opposition is not silenced. Why?
Because it rejects the known truth? This answer is
facile, uncharitable and improbable. Because of latent ethical bias? No doubt this plays its part. But
the answer is to be sought at a deeper level. We differ precisely as Protestant and Catholic must differ,
not on some single point of exegesis, nor on one or
two dogmas however important; we differ on our approach to the Word of God.

This profound difference lies beneath the surface
quarrel about our Lady's perpetual virginity. We
may lay our finger on it if we consult the *Church
Times* for 18 August, 1950. The impending definition of the dogma of the Assumption drew the following declaration from the Archbishops of Canterbury and York. The statement is admirably clear:

> There is not the smallest evidence in the Scripture
> or in the teaching of the early Church of belief in
> the doctrine of her bodily assumption. The Church
> of England refuses to regard as requisite for sav-
> ing faith any doctrine or opinions which are not
> *plainly* contained in the Scriptures.

In quoting this statement we are not wandering from
our subject for, singular as the doctrine of the Assumption may at first appear in that our historical
sources take us back only to the seventh century, yet
it differs only in degree from our present case, the
perpetual virginity, which is traceable only to the

third century and was not formally defined until the seventh.[8] And we have called attention to the word 'plainly' because, had it been omitted, a Catholic might have let the sentence stand.

Does the Bull *Munificentissimus* flatly contradict the whole of the statement from York and Canterbury? It does not. It draws no immediate argument from an explicit text of Scripture [9] nor does it claim to find the doctrine in the works of the most ancient Fathers. Instead, it takes two explicit *data* of the New Testament, the divine motherhood and our Lord's virginal conception, and upon these foundations builds the doctrine of the Assumption. The argument does not suppose for a moment that the doctrine is 'plainly' contained in the sense intended by the statement made on behalf of the Church of England—that is to say in the sense that the individual exegete could demonstrate the doctrine by using the rational tools of his trade. Of the above quotation it is therefore the second sentence with its significant adverb to which the Catholic outlook is opposed. The sentence rejects the Catholic conception of the controlled internal development of doctrine, of the *fecunda veritatis auctoritas,* an authority in which the conceived truth develops and is brought to birth.

We shall not be misunderstood, it is hoped, if we here register satisfaction that the gap between Catholics and others is now so clearly marked. Clear statement goes with true charity; there is nothing to be won by vagueness, nothing to be built in a mist.

One might fear the reaction of Protestants (one wrote on this occasion). . . . Their very 'scandal' shows us that it was not useless to make proclamation of our faith. The growing precision of Mary-dogma reveals the gap between us, no doubt, but it does not create the gap. If people could enter

---

[8] Cf. the Lateran Council of 649 (DB. 256; and cf. DB. 993).

[9] The phrase used in the Bull is: '. . . *Sacris Litteris tamquam ultimo fundamento nituntur,* in the last analysis having the Scriptures for its basis.'

the Church without believing in the Assumption of the Virgin and all that truth implies, it would be the beginning of a doctrinal crisis which would eventually erupt. Unity is never achieved or sustained by misunderstanding.[10]

The Council of Trent declared that the Church receives with equal veneration the sacred books and the apostolic traditions since both are expressions of the living Gospel, of the living Word which is the life-principle of the Christian and Apostolic Society. Now these two forms of expression in which the one Word of God makes itself heard, I mean the canonical books and the apostolic traditions, may be quantitatively complementary—one may speak where the other is silent. Whether this is in fact the case is open to discussion and is argued among Catholic theologians. But in any case all would be prepared to admit that the traditions are most often concerned not with adding to the content of the Writings, but with clarifying, synthesizing, applying that content.[11] If we are not to mislead the non-Catholic, therefore, it might be better to avoid the common formula: 'the two sources of Revelation'. Scripture and the apostolic traditions [12] are not two independent abso-

---

[10] *Revue Thomiste*, 1950, 2, 266f.

[11] The origin and practical purpose of the written Gospels (*aides-mémoire* of the early Christian preacher) and the incidental character of St Paul's surviving epistles might, at first thought, suggest that 'there are many things which are not written in this book' but which survive in the traditions. On the other hand, 'given the variety of the sacred writings which touch on so many religious themes, it is to say the least unlikely that any essential point of the divine message should have gone completely unmentioned'. (*Initiation Théologique*, 1, 81). We might add that even the decision on the canonical catalogue may be considered only as an explicitation of the apostolic commission recorded in the Scriptures — if we remember that 'apostolicity of origin' seems to have been the earliest criterion of canonicity.

[12] By 'apostolic traditions' we do not mean necessarily the passing on of formulae and facts absent from written Scriptures.

lutes, they interpenetrate and explain the one the other. With this in mind Newman wrote:

> I am not aware that later post-Tridentine writers deny that the whole Catholic faith may be proved from Scripture, though they would certainly maintain that it is not to be found on the surface of it, nor in such sense that it may be gained from Scripture without the aid of Tradition.[13]

Sacred Scripture, inspired as it is, of its nature is a fixed form with the shortcomings inherent in every fixture, but the Word of God of which Scripture is one expression is dynamic and actual. We cannot call the 'plain' sense of Scripture the end of God's continuous self-revealing process. Indeed, Man will never reach the end, for the Beatific Vision itself is an eternal progress endlessly astounding the blessed with new discovery. In this life too the fixed canonical utterance strives for further articulation. The eternal Word demands repeated concrete expressions appropriate to this or that human time while itself remaining the same.

The Protestant position, at least as it found expression in the Amsterdam Conference of 1948, leaves room for the development of the Word:

> The Protestant puts the emphasis upon the freedom of the Holy Spirit, upon God's repeatedly renewed initiatives by which, through his Word, he supervises, corrects, maintains, renews and cherishes his Church.[14]

A Catholic would not repudiate this view but, for him, the divine 'initiatives' are canalized through

The phrase implies the shape of the Church's living (Sacraments, moral practice and the like) outlined already in the apostolic age.

[13] *Development*, 7, 1, 3, 4.

[14] Cf. *Ephemerides Theologicae Lovanienses*, 1952, p. 684.

God's instituted Society by which also they are verified.[15] 'Bible and Bible only' is capable therefore of being a misleading formula for describing the non-Catholic bodies. They, too, demand what we may call the Biblical Complement but whereas for the Catholic the emphasis is upon its continuous and collective conveyance through the instituted Church, the Protestant envisages the Word conveyed sporadically and, as it were, immediately and individually. The choice of the neutral is, to use Barthian terms, between the Institution and the Event, between Catholic corporate Tradition and the inspiration of the individual, between the apostolic succession and a new series of prophets. Despite this fundamental difference it is nevertheless interesting to our subject that, if our judgment is correct, the principle of development is admitted in Continental Protestantism, that the 'plain' meaning of Scripture is capable of expansion.

We have said that the written Word, though a continual point of reference, is not the final goal. St Paul's own scrutiny and exposition of the 'deposit' shows that when he urged Timothy to keep it he was not thinking of gold in a chest but of a plant in soil. Even Paul's was an effort to express in the terms of his day and circumstances the powerful new divine reality which could exhaust that vocabulary and leave infinitely more to be said. For it is true that the New Testament itself, undeviating compass though it is, sets no limit to our way. 'The nature of the New Testament is entirely misunderstood if we lose sight of its true character which is one of effort towards the perfect expression of a new truth (i.e., of the revelation of God in the flesh), of the movement of thought towards a peak, a thought which, as day succeeds day, demands more precise expression.[16]

[15] This is not to deny God's initiatives in the isolated soul of the non-Catholic of good faith who thus belong 'unknowingly, initially, tendentially to the Church'.

[16] J. Levie, S.J., *Nouvelle Revue Théologique*, 1949, p. 1008.

It is this movement of thought, this effort towards complete synthesis, that the Church must continue from century to century, and each Christian within the Church. It is true that revelation in its entirety was given in the apostolic age, but it was given—as the divine pedagogy dictated—in order to be made more explicit, to achieve formulation and synthesis in the Church and by the Church. The Church, indeed, declining the false compliment offered her by Modernism, refuses to be regarded as a factory of new dogmas; and yet she could never tolerate an attitude like Tyrell's: 'If you can live on the undeveloped germ you may dispense with developments, especially if they but puzzle and hinder you.' [17]

A practical corollary follows to which Père Levie calls attention in the article just quoted. He expresses surprise at the ease with which certain exegetes and theologians declare this or that theological doctrine 'formally taught in the Scriptures'. And all too often the private Catholic exegete is expected to demonstrate with arguments sought from syntax and context the elaborated doctrine of the twentieth century, as if the inspired writers had not used the idiom of their own time; is expected, in other words, to turn uncompromisingly Protestant, to defend a position he indignantly repudiates and make mere logic fecundate the textual ovum. Now the true state of the case is that the Church's consciousness of the Word within her has become progressively sharper: the Spirit has been and is doing its work. What the Church did not perceive the day before yesterday she perceived yesterday. This consciousness, not blind and creative but objectively analytic, increasingly penetrates the committed Word. And this Word is not abstract to be thought, but vital to be lived: so for example the Word of the Cross grows daily more articulate as the Church repeatedly represents, re-presents, sacramentally assimilates the crucified Word.

The Church's knowledge of the Word, then, is not

[17] *A Much-Abused Letter*, p. 86.

merely equal to the sum of the Biblical scholarship of twenty centuries. It vastly exceeds it, or rather transcends it because it is of another sort. The equation: Logic *plus* Text *equals* Theology is quite inadequate in the Catholic view because it leaves out the *Spiritus suggeret omnia,* the Spirit will bring all to your mind that I have spoken to you (John 14:26); that was not idly said. The God-given synthesis does not violate logic but neither is it limited by logic; and that is why, even granted that in fact all necessary truths are to be found in the Scriptures, Driedo could say more than four hundred years ago that not every heresy can be confuted from Sacred Scripture.[18] Thus, for we must take an example, a scholar may accept the authenticity and immediate implication of the Petrine texts and yet feel uncompelled by historical or logical argument to deduce the Papal prerogative.[19] His attitude is not dishonest; it remains 'reasonable' so long as he puts no faith in the living Tradition. 'He who does not accept this faith will easily find exegetical and historical difficulties which legitimate his refusal; he who accepts it does not do so without assurance as complete as human knowledge is capable of furnishing.'[20] The Petrine texts provide a basis, a foundation, suggesting the outlines of the building, but to appreciate their full significance it is necessary not only to have seen the building but to have lived in it. The Tradition, in this case the legitimately emerged and emerging form of Church government, must be lived if the Word which it interprets is to be known. And that is the answer to the frequently recurring problem of the non-Catholic scholar's refusal of Catholic biblical interpretations.

The term 'inspired' has become almost a monopoly

[18] *Ephemerides Theologicae Lovanienses,* 1950, p. 44.

[19] So O. Cullmann, *Peter: Disciple, Apostle, Martyr* (London, 1953).

[20] Cf. Review of the above by Benoit, *Revue Biblique,* 1953, pp. 565-579.

of the Sacred Books. This is possibly unfortunate.
It is true that the Scriptures are 'the excelling, inspired and essential expression of the Faith'; nevertheless we must beware of a narrow and inexact idea
of Inspiration. 'Inspiration is in fact a rich *charisma*
of which Scriptural Inspiration is only one, and not
the highest, kind. Beside it, and superior to it, are
Prophetic and Apostolic Inspiration—*charismas* directed not to writing down the revelation but to its
budding forth in the richness of its first oral forma-
tion and to the many sided development of the revelation in a living community chosen by God to
elaborate and transmit the Word'.[21] This is what
Newman meant by 'the Prophetical Tradition existing primarily in the bosom of the Church herself' or
'pervading the Church like an atmosphere'.[22]

Now this 'Inspiration' or this 'Tradition' is not to
be conceived only, though this it is also, as a check
or brake upon religious thought and practice. It is a
positive driving force. Hence, as Père Benoit notes,
it is a mistake to describe even Infallibility as a negative *charisma* preserving from error. On the contrary, it is a positive *charisma* which makes the
Church better perceive and declare in the course of
time the truth implicitly contained in the apostolic
rule of faith. To this remark we may add, since it is
connected with it, that dogmatic definition is not to
be viewed as unhappy necessity compelled by heresy
and grudgingly accepted by the Church at large.
What heresy stimulated the definition of the Assumption? The Church is not a nervous mistress of exegesis, fearful lest the text breaks in her hands. She
claims the Spirit of Christ who 'spoke as one having
authority' and in that Spirit she finds not survival
only but exuberant life.

What precisely does this Spirit confer in the order
of the Church's knowledge? It is a matter of experience that the higher intelligence tends to arrive at

[21] *Revue Biblique*, 1955, pp. 258-264.
[22] *Development*, 2, 2, 2.

the unity behind plurality, to achieve the faculty of seeing many things in one idea. Now though they had received the totality of Truth (which is the *Mysterium Christi*) the Apostles did not live to see the refraction of that ray through the prism of time which was to give the Church opportunity to live the revealed Word by sacrament and devotional thought. Diversity grew from the primitive unity because the revelation accorded in its fullness to the Apostles was not a series of theological propositions but a concrete perception of the fact of Christ, of the total reality of redemptive work.[23] Rather it is not so much that multiplicity has grown from unity as that the unique has been, is being, more deeply sounded. In the higher synthesis which is the fruit of the spirit and not the conclusion of syllogistic process the Church sees, but does not forge, the link between text and dogma, dogma and further dogma.

So for the Mary-doctrine, glory of our age. The virginal conception, the divine motherhood, Immaculate Conception, bodily Assumption and amongst these Mary's perpetual virginity—all are an extension of the *Mysterium Christi*. The statement must seem extravagant to those who demand logical and historical demonstration, though it is salutary for all to remember how the adoption of the title *Theotokos* in the fifth century secured for ever a right faith in the manhood of the eternal Son. The Catholic, who believes that the Church's intuition is of the promised Spirit, knows that the privileges of Mary are the outworks of the central fortress which is Christ. And indeed it is historical fact, as Newman notes, that the early heresies though opposite to each other all tended remarkably to her exaltation. The Catholic theologian does not apologize for this great Mary-ward thrust; he welcomes it not for its own sake alone but because it illustrates the specifically Catholic principle we have described: that Scripture is formally insufficient.

[23] H. de Lubac, *Recherches de Sciences Religieuses*, 1948, p. 155.

The responsibility for supplying for this insufficiency is assumed by, because it was committed to, the Society of Christ which we call the Church. We have tried to show that it must be assumed by someone and the charge is not yet answered that the Reformation merely set up one infallibility in place of another: the infallibility of the Book (which means of the scholar or of isolated *illuminés* so often at variance) for an infallible Church. The individual conservative Protestant pastor and his liberal neighbour each takes upon himself the responsibility for his flock and freely decides if his interpretation of the Word is correct or not. But the Catholic declines to commit himself to this individualism. Before his eyes it is the corporate Church that expands the Word. And she, notably in our age, boldly displays the privileges of Mary. They are founded indeed upon the great Scriptural *datum* of her virginal motherhood and not contradicted by rational interpretation of the Written Word but they are discerned in their separateness, like rolling hills as the dawn brightens, only by the light of her Spirit. In her the Word grows. She is the soil. In the Mass for the spread of the true faith we pray that the Word may advance, ever declaring itself more clearly: *Sermo currat et clarificetur.*

CHAPTER 12

The Inspired Word

THOSE who oppose the cause of Christ dogmatically or morally, eagerly or under duress, outnumber at this present time those who sustain it. There is at least one happy result. Christians are beginning to realize that the differences which keep them from each other, however important, are small compared with their common isolation from the anti-Christian world. It is therefore vital that we should not through ignorance of each other imagine differences that do not exist or exaggerate those that do. Nothing is to be gained by mutual misunderstanding. Moreover, if a start is to be made, it must be at the right end. I mean that spectacular results may be achieved by *rapprochement* on the social, or even juridical, plane; but these will not be lasting unless there is agreement, even agreement to differ, on a far deeper level. The following chapter is an attempt to understand the Christian thinking of others than Catholics on a subject that seems of all the most promising and, save one that we shall mention, the most fundamental. For to the pagan the Catholic goes empty-handed; to the Jew with half a book; to other Christians with the whole of it. It is the common consent of Christendom that the Bible is a locus of divine authority, a sphere of divine revelation. We can hardly overstate the significance of this common admission; it is so much more important than many dividing differences. It is true that we appear to differ, even here, on the source and nature and effects of this Book's authority but, perhaps more often than not, our so-called differences are no more than variant emphases, interpretations peculiar to a theologian or to a school of theology, or even out-and-out misunderstandings of respective positions.

It is the urgent business of this generation to break through all such barriers, hitherto so effective and yet so often illusory. After this has been done there will no doubt be left some incompatibility. I am cowardly enough to suggest that we bequeath this problem to our children, but sufficiently bold to prophesy that the incompatability will be found elsewhere and not precisely here—that is to say, not precisely in our view of the nature of Scriptural Inspiration but in our varying conceptions of the nature and function of Christ's Church.

It would be idle and inconclusive to patch our quarrels without identifying their underlying cause. Now the rise of Protestantism coincided with a return to the Biblical text: this was to be expected as a result of the new Biblical perspective of the Reformers. Moreover, the refusal of the Vulgate version dictated recourse to the original languages. The results were far-reaching and not always unfortunate. It is scarcely extravagant to trace back to this development a perception—or, better, an assimilation—of the Hebrew mind less marked in those whom historical accident had forced to accept Greek formulations that substituted the abstract for the Semitic concrete. Now—as we have seen—the Hebrew does not think in propositions; he certainly does not think of God in propositions; nor did he think of God-given propositions. His God is the God who acts, not who argues. The Hebrew thinks in existential terms rather than in those of an essentialist philosophy. So also in the New Testament neither John nor Paul, for example, develops a theology of essences: they seek no metaphysical explanation of the mystery of Christ: their attention is focused on his mission, not on the analysis of his personality. So John gives to Jesus the names: 'Logos', 'Light', 'Life'; his theology and Christology are functional.

For those with an exclusively biblical outlook, an essential analysis of the Written Word is no less unnatural and unscriptural than an essential analysis of the Incarnate Word. Modern Protestantism, it is true, confesses that for centuries its adherents fell into the trap; that what Brunner calls the 'frozen waterfall' of post-Lutheran Protestantism was a sad departure from the fresh intuitions of Luther and Calvin, and a subsidence into the *rigor scholasticus*. Nevertheless it claims, not unfairly, that this was a betrayal of its own nature and hails Barth and Brunner as its faithful and articulate exponents. It is held that Bartha's theology of the Word, the Word dynamic, operative, efficacious, is the needed corrective for the intellectualist approach. For Barth, the Word is an event (Brunner uses the term 'encounter'), a divine impact upon the Bible reader; the Word is not just an authority guaranteeing doctrine; its primary quality is that of a living, a vital act by which God in person comes to us. It is creative and omnipotent and therefore free; nor can it be conceived separately from the person of Christ. Against this background must be seen, and understood, the tendency to speak of Revelation [1] and Authority rather than of Inspiration. With this tendency there goes a fear that the Bible, regarded as a speech about God, may itself become the object of faith; that the term 'revelation' be equated with 'doctrine', and the word 'faith' be completely identified with an assent of the intellect.

But where unmodified intellectualism operates, the only valid and real reason for distinguishing between revelation and doctrine, between the act of revealing and what the Church teaches, collapses. Ontologically they are indistinguishable. There is no longer a distinction to be drawn between the communication by God of Himself and the communication of truths concerning God; revelation and doctrine are no longer different things. The path is thus neatly prepared for the

---

[1] It should be understood that by 'revelation' is meant not the communication of an abstract truth but a powerful and personal divine impact.

identification of God's revelation and the Church's teaching.[2]

The complaint is thus diagnosed by A. G. Hebert:

The difficulty that has arisen over the conception of Revelation in the western tradition of Christendom has been due to the rationalizing of the idea. Where the Bible gives us concrete eschatological imagery and existential thinking, western thought has tended first to a philosophical mode of rationalization whereby imagery has been systematized into doctrines, and faith has been treated as an assent to doctrines. It has tended next to a scientific rationalization which envisages only the 'literal' truth of natural science and history. In both cases Inspiration is necessarily rendered as Inerrancy. In the one case the inspired Scripture is incorporated into a theological system; in the other, it is understood as an infallible record of events.[3]

It is not difficult, therefore, to detect a haunting fear of Rome's 'intellectualism' in the Biblical realm and a mistrust of its analysis of the nature of the sacred books. And it may be that there is a salutary warning here. It is right that we should suspect emotionalism and individual intuitions, but no analysis of Inspiration should leave out of account the working of the Spirit through the Scriptures upon the soul. A philosophical analysis has indeed been enforced as a defensive measure; it has served its purpose but we need not admire it for its own sake. It was doubtless demanded by the nineteenth century attack which, like so many others in the Church's history, scored successes it had never planned. I mean that the attack upon Biblical inerrancy, repulsed more or

[2] J. K. S. Reid, *The Authority of Scripture* (London 1957), p. 116.

[3] A. G. Hebert, *The Authority of the Old Testament* (London 1947), pp. 100-101.

less successfully on the central front, so diverted the Catholic mind that the Bible may have seemed to become for it a series of propositions each anxiously awaiting vindication, and Inspiration an inflexible instrument of infallibility. What is taken to be the Catholic attitude on this matter of inerrancy is a source of such annoyance outside the Church that it is worth a little discussion.

It is commonly alleged that the scientific, historical, and textual progress made in the last century left the Catholic unperturbed. He rode the crisis blandly, murmuring to himself: 'The Bible is without error', as one who should say: 'My mind is made up; please do not confuse me with facts'. Meanwhile, these facts were threatening havoc: notably evolutionary theory and biblical literary criticism. The annoyance of those who watched the Catholic is easily explained: while they reckoned his position false, they envied his assurance in it, his confidence that all necessary guidance and interpretation were safe in the hands of Christ's society. With those who were not thus assured, it was otherwise. The appeal away from the Church which, whatever his original intentions, Luther eventually made, left his successors face to face with the danger of illuminism and, ultimately, of Liberalism. The Bible was naked to its friends as well as to its enemies. It became vital for Protestant orthodoxy to defend it, and the Lutheran honeymoon was followed by the sterner business of housekeeping. Intellectualism established itself where it was least expected: Scripture became less and less a personal revelation from God and more and more a series of propositions about God: the dogma of absolute inerrancy, rigid to the point of absurdity, followed. As we have said, the modern Protestant reaction has been violent—indeed it has recoiled from a paper pope as sharply as from a personal one. The Protestant of today demands that revelation be not reduced to syllogisms but left what it truly is—a personal impact of God. He is thus absolved from vindicating the Bible from error, for where there is no proposition there is neither error nor truth; impact may be effective or ineffective, it cannot be true or false.

How does this compare with the modern Catholic view? Here too there has been a revulsion, not from the principle of inerrancy but from abnormal preoccupation with it. There is a healthy movement away from what threatened to became an obsession, the result of an over-anxious defence. Catholics are now beginning to point out that inerrancy is not the purpose of Inspiration nor its only consequence, as it would have been had God inspired the sacred books solely with the purpose of teaching truths. But in fact the sacred writers, and therefore God himself, more often than not set out to work upon the heart and emotions rather than to teach truth. And it is interesting that scholastic distinctions are now being employed to bring us back to the unscholastic Semitic mind of the original writers, to remind us that when we say: 'The Bible is true', we mean primarily what the Hebrew would mean. For the Hebrew does not look at truth in exactly the same way as the Latin or the Greek. To the Greek mind, pursuing absolute clarity, that is true which is unveiled, delivered from darkness. For the Latin, soaked in juridical principle, that is true whose authority is guaranteed. For a Hebrew that is true which has been put to the trial and found solid; for him, truth is not opposed to error but to lies, and to what he calls 'vanity', that is to say, what is lacking in durability and solidity. It is in this sense that his God is the God of truth—the one upon whom he could always rely. In the Bible, the symbol of truth is not so much 'light' and 'rock', and the Hebrew *'emeth* from the root *'amen* expresses security, it is used of one who carries a child safely.[4] For the Hebrew, therefore, the truth of his Scriptures is their dependability as God's word, that is, as God's *pledged* word, his promise which he will certainly fulfil.

[4] Cf. J. Guillet, *Thèmes Biblique*, Paris, 1954, pp. 38-42.

All this it is well to remember. Nevertheless, the Catholic cannot accept the suppression of the intellect in the Barthian manner. True to the basic principles of the Reform, or rather of what Bouyer calls their negative counterparts (denial of the efficacy of divinely informed work and sacrament; refusal of substanital change in the soul of man) Barth's 'faith' is an affirmation, made in total darkness, of a God who cannot effectively come to man. God's word is therefore ineffable. This is more than paradox: it is dilemma. In reacting from intellectualism and seeking to recover the Semitic, integral outlook, we must not cut off man's head to save his heart. What has been called the 'embarrassing' adherence of Bultmann to the Barthian system shows us whither this system leads. There is no further need to verify any objective, historical working-out of a divine plan in the record of Scripture; there are no supernatural realities revealing God's will; man can receive no ideas of real value; faith is an existential decision of total abandonment to a word which he cannot of his nature begin to understand; but this unknown word he must accept in a blind act which is both liberating and saving. The Bible is a blind giant; a Samson with his eyes out. We are reduced to complete agnosticism and Christianity is no longer a historical religion and therefore no distinctive religion at all.

On the other hand, it is well for us to be on our guard against so misreading Inspiration's purpose as to seek in the inspired books a corpus of propositional doctrine formulated in the scholastic manner. One may quote with some approval the words of Austin Farrer:

In the case of the Trinity, the old scholastic way was to hunt for propositions declaring the doctrine in philosophical form; the new scholastic way is to classify texts with the same purpose. But all this is based on the false assumption that Paul and John, for example, had anything like a system on conceptual lines; they lived in fact with images, not with concepts; their interrelationships are those of images according to their own imagery laws and not according to the principles of a conceptual system. Moreover, the scholastic method is inconclusive in its results because it attempts to find the Trinity as a single scheme behind the images, whereas there is no scheme; we know that Paul speaks of a personal divine action of the Father, Son and Spirit, and that he was not a polytheist—but it is a risky inference from here to say that Paul was speaking of divine persons in their own right, and not perhaps of instrumental modes of the Father's action. We must not logically infer from images. The right method is to seek the image of the Trinity and its relationship to other images. . . . Only after this can we ask what metaphysical comment the New Testament image of the Trinity provokes and which subsequent theological conceptualizations do least violence to it.[5]

To these remarks we may add that, whatever certain manuals may regrettably imply, the Catholic Church does not claim merely to infer logically from the texts; in virtue of the Word living in her, she claims to propound the doctrine in terms of the prevailing thought-framework in such a way that she expresses, not indeed adequately (for this is impossible), but expresses infallibly in terms of one culture the Scriptural thought that was originally conveyed in terms of another.

But it is in our divergent attitudes to, or identifications of, authority that our deepest division might be expected to lie. The division is perhaps not as deep as it appears. It might be thought that the Reformers, Luther and Calvin, localized this authority in the pages of the Bible—and a case could be made out for this view. Yet it might be more exact to say that, for Calvin at least, the authority lies not in the

[5] A. Farrer, *The Glass of Vision*.

page but in Christ: the seat of the Bible's authority is outside itself. However this may be, the modern Protestant refuses either to identify Scripture with the Word of God or to invest the Scriptures with an external authority legalistically conceived. For him the Bible is the means elected by God's free grace for the operation of God's free grace; it is the chosen and accredited instrument of God. In Lutheran terms, the Bible is the crib in which Christ is laid; its authority is Christ himself. 'Revelation (and by this, we repeat, is meant not intellectual enlightenment but divine impact) is not to be *identified* with Scripture. As Barth says, Revelation is the objective entity to which proclamation is related and without which proclamation would be simply heart-searching—the 'endless monologue' which the Catholic Church is accused of holding with itself. In standing before Scripture, it is said, we do not stand before authority itself—rather we stand before that in which, as we hear it, we hear God himself speaking. The authority of Scripture is not a possession of Scripture nor even a gift bestowed upon it by God himself. Scripture is authoritative because God himself takes it and speaks through it.[6]

Behind all this, which may seem to us very anxious pleading, there are — I think — two disposing causes: one is a reaction from the fundamentalist Protestant Orthodox position which modern scholarship has made untenable; the other is a reaction from a mistaken view of the Roman claim. The first of these is not our immediate concern, though it may be suggested that here the recoil from Protestant Orthodoxy has perhaps gone a little too far—all that was needed was a more supple conception of Inspiration than the Orthodox Protestant would admit. The second disposing cause springs from a desire to safeguard the free sovereignty of God who can bind himself to no printed page, and certainly not to any human institution. It is objected that the Roman

[6] On this, cf. Reid *op cit.*, pp. 215 and 221.

Church, regarding the Scriptures as a *depositum* to be interpreted by the Church herself, sins against this sovereignty. Barth presents us with the choice between an autonomous, self-governing Church, and a Church obedient to an authority over against itself, namely to God's authority wielded in the Scriptures. The Catholic will reply that a third alternative is possible, namely of a Church which is not simply a gathering of human beings either self-governing or acknowledging an authority outside itself, a Church that is itself the living and extended Christ whose authority remains, not because he commits it to men but because he gathers men into himself. In this, as in so many other disputes, we are brought back to the old statement that the problem perpetually unresolved in Protestantism is the problem of the Church. For the Catholic, the Scriptures are the voice of the Word pre-incarnate, incarnate, post-incarnate: the locus of authority has never shifted. The Church cannot usurp because the Church is Christ and Christ is the Word. This being so, it is surely wide of the mark to accuse Catholicism of turning the dynamic Word into a dead deposit or of turning impact into proposition: the Word is alive in the Church — too alive according to some — becoming ever more articulate; and the Word is lived in the Church, securing its impact by sacrament and sacrifice.

We may now come at last to the question of Inpiration's nature. Like certain other excursions into speculative theology the quest for a *definition* of Inspiration may be described as a regrettable necessity. But we cannot ignore the fact that, though the question may be the wrong one it cries for an answer — whatever future ages have to say about the futility of the discussion. We have said that non-Catholic scholars are more eager to speak of Authority than of Revelation, that is to say, to speak existentially rather than essentially—and this is perhaps the more profitable way and may lead them to unexpected places in the end. Yet our different approaches cross from time to time and we meet attempts at essential definition. All are agreed, for instance, that Inspiration makes the Bible a unique book, though when we ask in what precisely this uniqueness consists we are answered variously. Barth explains that the Bible, which has no *efficacia extra usum,* no intrinsic quality independent of the reader, is unique in this, namely that it is the sole God-chosen occasion of his self-revelation. In it from time to time God allows himself to be the object of human language; it is within this chosen sphere that the event-of-the-Word occurs; the Bible is God's Word only insofar as God lets it speak; the Bible and Revelation are distinct but become one in the Event. The uniqueness of the Bible is not locked up in the past, it is bestowed freely by God in the present and will be in the future. This view is well expressed by Reid:

> The Bible does not contain the Word of God as in a sack; God marches up and down through the Bible magisterially, making his word come to life at any point through its length and breadth. The Bible becomes the Word of God by stated and steady appointment. It is the named place where God confronts man.[7]

We cannot but applaud Barth's positive contribution to the whole question. The Word is indeed not tied down to the past, nor restricted to cold print, nor primarily intellectual; it is free, and its causality is physical and immediate. But in the Barthian position as a whole there appears to be a forced emphasis deriving from wider principles. In the first place, the old Nominalism of the Reform period is lurking in it. It is held that, just as the *gratia gratum faciens,* the grace that makes a man acceptable to God, which we call sanctification can change nothing intrinsic in men, so the *gratia gratis data,* given freely for the public good, that we call Inspiration is not,

[7] J. K. S. Reid, *op. cit.,* p. 278.

and cannot be, an insertion of the divine into the human: God cannot commit himself to anything human (though we might observe that even in Barth's account God has committed himself to a human *sphere* of activity, otherwise the uniqueness of the Bible goes altogether). This outlook cannot tolerate the idea of God assuming a human tool and making it truly his own. Secondly, there is the old fear of a propositional deposit which might seem to be demanded if the Word is committed to every and each sentence of the Scriptures. Thirdly, there is—as Bouyer points out[8]—the immense political value of the Barthian perception; it extricates Institutional Protestantism from its dilemma: on the one hand, the concept of the Word imprisoned in a book without court of appeal (leading either to Illuminism or to Liberalism); on the other hand (the only alternative), an appeal to external authority. This external authority that might fatally have been the Church was in fact supplied by Barth—modern Protestantism at last had its alibi; Barth found the authority in neither page nor pope but in the Word itself, or better 'himself', the Word not imprisoned nor identified with the Bible but utterly transcendent, ranging free.

How does the prevailing Catholic theory escape the charge of the Word contained in the Scripture as in a sack? How does it escape the charge of a propositional deposit, of a Bible that is nothing less than a series of *ex cathedra* pronouncements, a block of dogmatic homogeneous density? It may be that the Franzelin hypothesis of ideas from God, words from man, could so have been indicated. Indeed, it is this theory, one fears, that may have misled some of our opponents; but the theory has not in fact survived. Instead, most Catholics accept in its main outlines the theory of a willing and thinking tool preserving freedom and personality even in

[8] L. Bouyer, *The Spirit and Forms of Protestantism* (London, 1956), pp. 241-242.

the act of being moved mysteriously by God. Consequently, not only do the words truly belong to the human author but the ideas too; and these ideas, like the words, retain their human limitations and their contingent character and, as a result, their potentiality for development. There is no imprisonment of the Word who freely moves his instruments; it is true that he accepts the limitations of human language even as he accepted the limitations of human flesh, but he reserves the right to outstrip the limitations by miracle in one case and by spiritual impact in the other. The Word does not cease to dwell in the written word; the writing is a continued incarnation and the written word is always the potent fringe of the garment. Here, too, the Word remains free, and virtue goes out from him only at his will. In this sense we can say with Barth that the Bible becomes the Word in the fullest sense when this impact-event takes place within this chosen sphere of revelation. The impact is upon the individual, of course, but it affects primarily the society founded by and upon the Word. This impact touches and develops the living of that society which progressively penetrates the intentions of the Word, lives what it perceives and perceives what it lives—and what it perceives is not so much the single sentence as the total drive of the Word. Thus the sacramental system itself is the outcome of an integration of body and soul that is entirely characteristic of the Scriptures. Hence daily, and as it were domestically, the power of the Bible works upon those who may be ignorant of the text of the Bible and the Word works freely upon the individual soul.

But as for the *charisma* of Inspiration itself, one fears that behind the Protestant principle of Sacred Scripture as the decisive and unique expression of the Word of God there lies too exclusive an understanding of what Inspiration is. For if we are to judge, as we must judge, from the phenomena of our revealed religion, a multiple issue of the Spirit's activity is to be observed. It is evident, for instance, and happily emphasized in these days, that our Synoptic gospels did not spring into existence but rather crept. Their final committal to writing was the work of individuals moved by the Spirit: this movement we call Scriptural Inspiration.[9] But was the Spirit's activity so confined? What of the thirty years and more when the necessary preliminary work was going on in the early community? Can we not speak of Inspiration here? And may we say to the Spirit: 'Thus far and no farther' when the last Apostle dies? Revelation—by which we mean here the divulging of new supernatural truths — doubtless reached its fullness at this point, but how could the Spirit be idle when there was so much of that profound revelation still to be understood?

The question of criterion cannot, of course, be divorced from the problem of the nature of Scriptural Inspiration: to speak of 'a search for "x" ' is meaningless; I must know what I am looking for if I am to recognize it when found. Different conceptions of Inspiration, therefore, will mean different views on its criterion. Let us then be content with a highest common factor, and ask: 'How do we recognize that the Bible is *unique* among books?'

The historical fact that the Protestant movement sprang from Luther's 'vital intuition' of the religious truth imposed by the Scriptures, in particular by the Epistle to the Romans, has proved to be the father of many unexpected children. Thus, there is an anxiety—which is not confined to Protestant circles — to exclude the fully 'extrinsic' criterion which Catholics (wrongly, as I think) are credited with seeking. It is true that there is a healthy movement away from purely subjective criteria: the *gustus internus,* the inward satisfaction of the reader, has been rejected as plainly inadequate. On the other hand, it seems to be fairly widely agreed that the authority of a Church cannot of itself adequately

[9] On this, cf. Père Benoit's excellent review in *Revue Biblique* (1955), pp. 258-64.

commend the Bible—this is an inevitable affirmation for those whose view of the Church is not integrated. Thus, to take what may be called the middle way, the Report for Doctrine in the Church of England reads:

> Belief that the Bible is the inspired record of God's self-revelation to man and of man's response to that revelation is not for us a dogma imposed as a result of some theory of the mode of composition of the books[10] but a conclusion drawn from the character of their contents and the spiritual insight displayed in them.[11]

It is to be noticed that the proposed criterion is evidently intrinsic to the Book, though it has a certain objectivity. To the same line of thought belongs Farrer's criterion of pregnant images. Where this leads to may be seen from his answer to the objection that these images do not pervade the whole text of the Bible:

> To complain that apostolic inspiration was the germination of the image-seeds does not apply to the whole text and gives no plain account of the inspiration of the text of Scripture comparable with the old doctrine of inerrant supernatural dictation, is surely no blemish. For a doctrine of the unchallengeable inspiration of the whole text is a burden which our backs can no longer bear. What is vital is that we should have a doctrine of Scripture which causes us to look for the right things in Scripture.[12]

From this it would seem that an intrinsic criterion is regarded as insufficient to guarantee the unique-

---

[10] Apparently a circumlocutory indictment of what is taken to be the Catholic position.

[11] *Doctrine in the Church of England* (London, 1922), p. 27.

[12] A. Farrer, *The Glass of Vision.*

ness of the *whole* Bible—and this, after all, is the
common Christian datum. Nor is it true, as Farrer
seems to suggest, that the only alternative is that
revelation was given in the form of propositions.
'Inerrant supernatural dictation' is far from being a
definition of the supple Inspiration of which we have
spoken and which issues in many non-propositional
forms.

Barth's answer to the question of the Bible's recognizable uniqueness is that it is the work of witnesses, of prophets and apostles divinely appointed
whose position cannot be usurped by anyone else.
Brunner's reply is the same: the uniqueness of the
New Testament consists in this, that it is the witness
of the apostles who alone knew Christ without human intermediary. To this we might reply:

> The charisma of the Apostles as witnesses of
> Christ is indeed at the origin of all the fermenta-
> tion of the faith in the apostolic generation, but
> the Holy Spirit was working in others than the
> Apostles, namely in all the believers who were
> already the Church, and especially in the leaders
> whom God had chosen to build the Church, and
> who, acting under the guidance and stimulus of
> the Apostles, already constituted its first magis-
> terium. If we remember this concrete situation,
> we shall avoid making of the New Testament
> merely the written witness of the Apostles; and,
> on the other hand, we shall understand how this
> text could not contain all the potentialities of the
> apostolic witness in all its living quality and rich-
> ness.[13]

One may add that a criterion drawn from the situation and function of the writer is inadequate, because these things are not always known; indeed, the
complex origin of the Bible makes them unknowable: do we in fact know that each writer enjoyed

[13] P. Benoit, *loc. cit.*, p. 263.

a commission from either Synagogue or Church? Pressed by historical fact, Brunner says that the witness of the New Testament is borne by men, some of whom were eye-witnesses and also by 'others who stand in temporal proximity to them'. It is therefore necessary to conceive of the witness offered by the New Testament as having a wider basis than direct sight or hearing of the pre-Resurrection Christ. The witness has to be extended to those who experienced Christ risen and ascended — Paul himself is one of these. But why should we stop at Paul? The criterion is becoming very elastic, and Brunner is led to maintain that the Canon is neither final nor infallible, and that therefore the Church has the right and duty to revise it. He confesses, in short, the insufficiency of his criterion for the present accepted Canon.

Barth expresses his own conclusion thus:

> If the Achilles' heel of the Protestant system is the question: Who guarantees the divine character of Scripture? it may be said that the recognition of the authority of Scripture is a matter of confession and that, when this is realized, this very weakness is also Protestantism's greatest strength.[14]

Now this is interesting: this movement away from the old *gustus internus,* and now from the more objective but still intrinsic criterion, may well give us hope of understanding. For the Catholic would be the first to admit that the authority of Scripture is a matter of confession, the object of an act of faith, unproved and unproveable—because an affirmation of the supernatural order is necessary and alone adequate to establish a fact of the supernatural order. Apostolicity of origin did indeed play its part in delimiting the Canon, but the definition is made on the authority of the Word in the Church. This being so, it may be that we are misleading others if we refer

14 Quoted in Reid, *op cit.,* p. 218.

to an 'extrinsic' criterion; for in fact it is the same
Word that is the voice of the Scriptures and the
voice attesting the Scriptures. Here again we return
to the problem of the Church. The Scriptures are
recognized to be unique by the fact that the Word
speaking in the Church witnesses to the Word written in the Scriptures; no historical criterion of apostolicity will suffice as witness for that supernatural
fact.

We may ask, in conclusion, whether there has
been in recent years any signs of a growth in mutual
understanding, any approach to a rendezvous? The
answer is surely not in doubt. On the one side there
has been a retreat from the fundamentalist interpretation of Orthodox Protestantism; on the other side
there has been a recovery from undue preoccupation with inerrancy. Moreover, if ever there was a
Protestant principle of 'private judgment', it has gone
for good. 'Interpretation is the proprium of the
Church as a whole.' [15] 'It is now being understood
that the Bible is the book of the Israel of God and
that its several books must be read in the light of
the Tradition.' [16] Now, matching this advance towards Tradition on the non-Catholic side there is a
manifest return to the Bible on the part of Catholics
—it would be strange if we did not meet on the way
and perhaps begin to understand each other a little
better.

To others we would not presume to dictate a
course of action, but we may be allowed to make one
or two suggestions for our own procedure. We may,
for instance, be cautious with our words—mischief-
makers as they are. 'Verbal inspiration', writes C. H.
Dodd, 'maintains dictation by the deity. The books
consequently convey absolute truth with no trace of
error or relativity.'[17] Now, by 'Verbal Inspiration' we

15 Reid, *op. cit.*, p. 106.

16 Hebert, *op. cit.*, p. 308.

17 C. H. Dodd, *The Authority of the Bible* (London, 1947),
p. 35.

do not mean that at all, but since the phrase has served its turn — notably in the old Franzelin controversy—may we not allow it to drop out of its misleading existence? And perhaps the most unfortunate word of all has been 'revelation'. That Biblical revelation is mediated neither by syllogism nor by proposition does not mean that it is not at all concerned with the intellect, but so long as we continue to use the term for something primarily intellectual we shall not be understood by others and shall lose not a little ourselves.

And as for our doctrine of Scriptural Inspiration, it may be that analysis has done its defensive work and need go no farther. We must be sure, nevertheless, that our conception of it is not rigid; in this way we shall respect the racial mentality and the individual personality that God himself respected in his inspiring motion. We shall refrain from attributing to Paul or John a system of theology in line with a philosophy of essences; we shall allow for development of thought not only in the Old Testament but also in the New. So, for example, if Paul's outlook on widows changes, or if the notion of the *parousia,* of our Lord's 'coming', in John is not that which we find in the Pauline epistles, we shall not align two static propositions whose contrast is to be explained away; instead, we shall see two converging reactions to the same revelation. And this revelation we shall see rather as an event than as a coherent system of doctrine, as a succession of divine impacts on history and on historical personages—of whom the Bible's devout reader is one. We shall learn to concentrate less on the Bible as history (though this has its minor place), and more on the Bible as theology; less on the Bible as theology, more on the Bible as the story, and stories, of God's ways with men; less on the Bible as this story, more on the Bible as (by means of this story) the quasi-sacramental tool of God. For the Catholic biblical revival must not be allowed to exhaust itself in historical inquiry, equipping the enthusiast for Scriptural crossword-puzzles—as well take Baptismal water for the purification of pots and pans as so abuse this sacrament of the letter. We must read the Bible as it were on our knees.

And, finally, we must know the Church for what she is—the Body of the Word. She is most persistently accused of usurping what has in fact been given her, or rather what Christ has made her. It can only mislead those who misunderstand if we contrast the Word with the Body. One may therefore deprecate sentences like this: 'The Church is superior to the Bible in the sense that she is the living voice of Christ', for the Bible is the living voice of Christ, too, and so the living voice of the Church. The voice of the Word speaks in the hierarchy and masses of the living Church whose daily life, much more than the occasional pronouncement, is a continuing utterance of the Word whose Body she is.

Index